Rick Lamb's

Horse Smarts

FOR THE BUSY RIDER

ALSO BY RICK LAMB

The Revolution in Horsemanship and What It Means to Mankind
(with Robert M. Miller, D.V.M.)

Rick Lamb's

Horse Smarts

FOR THE BUSY RIDER

Insights in Small Bites from
The Horse Show Minute Radio Program

Rick Lamb
Foreword by Linda Parelli

THE LYONS PRESS
Guilford, Connecticut
An imprint of The Globe Pequot Press

The Lyons Press is an imprint of The Globe Pequot Press.

10 9 8 7 6 5 4 3 2 1

Printed in the United States of America

Photo on page 163 is by Heidi Nyland. All other photos © photos.com.

Library of Congress Cataloging-in-Publication Data

Lamb, Richard A.
  [Horse smarts for the busy rider]
  Rick Lamb's horse smarts for the busy rider : insights in small bites from the
horse show minute radio program / Rick Lamb.
      p. cm.
  Includes index.
  ISBN 1-59228-807-3
  1. Horses--Miscellanea. I. Title. II. Title: Horse smarts for the busy rider.
SF301.L333 2005
636.1--dc22
                                    2005027631

Contents

Acknowledgments

In this project, my first thanks must go to the guests on *The Horse Show with Rick Lamb*. By slicing and dicing their words into short sound bites, I was able to create the heart of each of my minute programs, and that was always where my own writing found its inspiration.

Of course, without my sponsors, affiliate stations, and listeners, I wouldn't be doing this today, so thanks go to them, too.

I want to offer an especially big thank-you to Susan Bolin, Director of Affiliate Relations for my radio shows. Syndicated radio can be a tough, cold business and Susan is a ray of light and warmth and optimism for all of us.

Likewise, senior recording engineer Jim Sherry is an inspiration, both professionally and personally.

To Linda Parelli, thanks for the foreword and for all you and Pat have given us.

To my editor, Steve Price, and the entire team at The Lyons Press, thank you for believing in me. Steve's first reaction to my work ("Egad, man. You're a <u>writer!</u>") is still pinned to my bulletin board.

My sons, Ryan and Todd, deserve special mention. I had the pleasure of working with each of them at my studio before they went on to their careers. For all of 2004, Ryan helped with countless computer chores related to my radio shows in order that I might have time to write. Thanks, guys. I'll always remember those times.

My stepdaughter, Blair, transcribed hundreds of my minute programs into computer text files to kick off this project. It was a tedious job, even for a bright teenager with ninety-wpm typing skills. Thanks, sweetie.

My final thanks must again go to my wife, Diana. I'm sure her life would have been easier if she'd married a nine-to-five kind of guy. I don't think she'd be any happier, though. I know I wouldn't.

—Rick Lamb
May 2005

Foreword

If you are as passionate about horses as me—and especially if you're dedicated to the self-development it takes to become a horseman—you're going to enjoy this book.

Rick is a phenomenal interviewer who has a talent for getting us to say meaningful things into a microphone. He's taken these pearls of wisdom and put them into a book where we can read just one page at a time and be enriched; we actually get a peek into the thoughts of the horsemen we admire.

Being a part of the new revolution in horsemanship makes me sensitive to the integrity of the information offered to horse people today, and thanks to Rick's special interest in natural horsemanship, I can flip confidently to any page knowing that what I'll find there honors the horse as a friend and teacher of the highest order.

—Linda Parelli
June 2005

Preface

This book, I'll admit, is an odd one. Each page was originally a short radio program, words intended for the ear rather than the eye. It is one of life's nice little surprises that, bundled together, they also form a remarkably handy book.

The scripts are organized into categories, but there's no reason to read them in any particular order. Jump around to your heart's content. And if you're feeling really wild, listen to the original audio at www.TheHorseShow.com.

I hope you enjoy the book. If it finds a home in your carry-on bag or in the waiting room at your office or in your breakfast nook, I will be very well pleased. These short pieces are food for thought, and they're packed with nutrition. I think you'll be surprised at how satisfying they can be.

This book is dedicated to every human
who has been willing to reinvent himself
to become a better horseman.

CHAPTER ONE

Behavior

Dominance Games

In every herd of horses there is a hierarchy, from the most dominant individual to the most submissive.

Horses are programmed by nature to be herd animals, and they all understand the rules of living in a herd. Each horse is submissive to the horses above him in the pecking order. The late Ronnie Willis, famed Montana horseman, described how this plays out when a new herd is formed.

> You take ten head of strange horses, put them in a corral—they get to checking each other out. They feel of each other. Then they feel *for* each other. Then you see them kind of rubbing on each other's necks standing there, and their withers and one thing and another. And then pretty soon one of them will kind of squeal a little bit and I think what he's really saying there is, "Let's let the games begin. We're going to find out who's going to drive this tugboat."

Dominance is established when one horse is able to control the movement of another, either getting it to move or restricting it from moving.

Right or Wrong Behavior

Does your horse ever do the wrong thing? Well, according to top clinician John Lyons, that's impossible.

Right or wrong, good or bad, correct or incorrect—these are human concepts that mean nothing to a horse. When we give a horse a cue, he responds in the only way his brain allows him to. John Lyons, "America's Most Trusted Horseman," explains it this way:

> The horse doesn't understand the difference between right and wrong. He only understands in terms of what *is*. If I kick and he does a behavior after that, whatever that behavior is, he thinks that's what he's supposed to do. He doesn't think in terms of this is right behavior and this is wrong behavior.

On the other hand, a horse may be conditioned to respond to a given stimulus in a predictable way, kind of like Dr. Pavlov's famous salivating dog. Conditioned response is at the heart of John Lyons's popular training methods.

Space Invaders

We humans like it when our animals want to be close to us, but horses that invade our personal space are dangerous.

With horses we have to enforce a double standard. It's okay for us to enter their personal space whenever we want to—but they are not to enter ours without an invitation. One of Aussie trainer Clinton Anderson's students learned this lesson the hard way.

> She was letting the horse invade her space at a clinic in Missouri, and she was hugging on it and kissing it and so forth. She was confused about why I wanted her to make the horse stay out of her space. And I said, "Because it's dangerous. Because if the horse gets fearful or disrespectful, it weighs a lot more than you. You're 150 pounds, so if it lands on you or runs over you, it's really going to hurt." And she said, "I don't think she'd do that to me." Ten minutes later the horse got a fright and just mowed her down.

What is your personal space? Clinton defines it as a four-foot radius circle around you. He calls it your hula hoop.

🐎 Curious Horse

It's good for a horse to be curious because curiosity exercises the thinking side of his brain.

A horse's natural curiosity is often inhibited by skepticism and fear of being hurt. That makes the first order of business building up his confidence in you. Approach and retreat is a good way to do that. Then you have to provide something that engages his interest. Popular horseman Pat Parelli explains:

> How do you get a horse to be curious? You've got to have not approach and retreat, but retreat. Why do horses get porcupine quills in their noses? Because the thing waddles away from them. This is what causes curiosity: things that go away and waddle and have a curious manner.

Pat uses this principle to get a loose horse to come to him. He crouches and moves toward the hindquarters to get the horse's attention. Then he straightens and walks backward, beckoning the horse to follow . . . and the horse does.

Finger in Mouth

Does it annoy you when your horse is constantly playing with his bit? It shouldn't. It keeps him happy!

Endorphins are those natural chemicals that create a feeling of well-being for marathon runners and other athletes. Science has proven that horses generate endorphins, too, but not in the same way. Believe it or not, movement of the horse's tongue, whether licking, chewing, or just playing with his bit, causes endorphin release. Trainer Richard Shrake talks about one way we can use this fact.

> I used to work for a gaited trainer, and it was fun, because every time these colts would stop, lock up, and just quit—not move—you know what he'd have us do? We'd reach down, put a finger in his mouth, and it was like starting an old-time car. As soon as he'd lick those lips, boom, this horse broke in the poll, lifted his shoulders, and trotted off.

So if your horse stalls, you have the key to restarting him right in your hand.

Yawning and Eye Rolling

What is a horse really feeling when he yawns or rolls his eyes? It's not always what you'd think.

Horses communicate with each other using a language of gestures that can involve various parts of the body. In his film, *Such is the Real Nature of Horses*, photographer Robert Vavra captured some unusual primitive behavior among horses that taught him, and the scientists with him, a thing or two about equine communication. One of the surprises was the use of the yawn.

> Horses usually yawn because of anxiety. In the film you see a stallion passing another stallion who has a mare in estrus. As the foreign stallion passes, the other one looks at him and yawns twice. And we saw this again and again.

Another surprise was the use of eye rolling. Instead of indicating fear, as we might expect, it was observed to be a threatening gesture when used between horses.

Looking a Horse in the Eye

Eye contact is very powerful when working with a horse, but you may be surprised at the effect that it can have.

Horses communicate with each other using gestures that form a language clinician Monty Roberts calls Equus. Humans can use this language too, but it can be very foreign to us. For instance, Monty says that when you look your horse in the eye, you're telling it to go away. Some people have a hard time accepting this.

> People just don't seem to understand that, because we anthropomorphize to the extent that we human beings want to be able to look our horse in the eye just as we look our friends in the eye when we speak with them. And we think, "Well, it's rude to look away when you're having a conversation." And they'll often say to me, "When can I look my horse in the eye and not have it go away?" Well, you want to change the language now? That's fifty million years of age.

According to Monty, dropping your eyes away is the correct gesture for inviting your horse to come to you.

Subordinate as Prey

Take a look at the dynamics between a trainer and a horse. It's not that different from what you see in the workplace.

Canada's top equine behaviorist is clinician Chris Irwin, an unusually creative and articulate teacher. Besides helping people with their horses, Chris has found that his observations on horse behavior have direct application in the office. He explains:

> Whenever two human beings are relating and one person is in the power position, that makes the other person the prey, the victim—the horse. I'm the CEO and I'm trying to get something out of my vice president of marketing. I need him to do his job better, so psychologically, how we approach that really is not unlike how a good trainer would approach a horse.

Chris points out that body language is key and must be consistent, not only with what is said, but with the speaker's intent as well.

Watching a Horse's Eye

No matter how quick your reflexes, you can't get out of the way once a horse starts to kick you, and you shouldn't try.

You are no match for a horse. He weighs five to ten times what you do, and he's much stronger and faster. So how do you protect yourself from being kicked or bitten? Trainer Clinton Anderson discovered the secret while working with brumbies, the wild horses of his native Australia.

> Watch their eye. Their eye will light up. Everything that happens with their body or their legs comes from their eye first. Like if I'm worried about a horse kicking me, I don't look at their leg, because by the time I look at their leg, it's already in my belly. So if you can get quick enough to read that, you can adjust your position to make sure that you're not in any danger.

A horse may also lay his ears back before striking, but this is more a sign of effort than aggression. Horses often pin their ears when playing or working and they're not upset about anything. If you want a good indicator of what's on your horse's mind, the eyes have it.

Fear of Cattle

A top cow horse can bring his rider fame and fortune in the show pen, but what makes a good cow horse?

No one is a greater authority on the Western performance horse than multi-time world champion Al Dunning of Arizona. His ability to breed and train horses that excel at working a cow is legendary. Al looks for horses that want to play with the cow, rather than chase it and bite it. And surprisingly, some of the best cow horses he's ever had started out frightened of cattle.

> The greatest horse I ever rode in my life was Expensive Hobby, and he was totally afraid of cattle. I had to spend lots of time riding him around the herd and that kind of stuff. You'd ride him to a cow and that cow would move; he'd blast off that cow and I'd stop him, ride him back up, and he ended up learning the pattern and learning control. He was a great reiner and a great cow horse, and then he ended up being a great cutting horse.

For Al, it's about the horse's athleticism and trainability.

A Horse's Memory

You've probably heard it said that an elephant never forgets. Well, remember this: A horse doesn't forget, either.

Dr. Robert M. Miller has pioneered the training of newborn foals with a procedure he calls imprint training. The training is highly effective because one, it takes place when the horse is able to learn easiest and fastest, right after birth. And two, like horses of any age, a foal will remember what he learns for the rest of his life. This remarkable memory is a trait the horse shares with another very different species. Dr. Miller explains:

> Having done zoo work throughout my career, I can say that the two outstanding memories in the animal kingdom are the elephant and the horse. In the case of the horse, you have to remember when to run in order to stay alive. So horses have a phenomenal memory, and there's no time lapse. They memorize something that impresses them, good or bad; ten years go by, it's still there.

Four Steps to Learning

Just how important is it for a horse to feel safe? According to experts, all learning depends upon it.

Horses can think of only one thing at a time, and since they're prey animals, they're most often thinking about their own survival. To free their brains to process what we're trying to teach them, we've got to make them feel safe, as the late Montana horse trainer Ronnie Willis explained.

The way that he learns is, number one from confidence, then acceptance, then understanding, and then the achievement—the result. And if you play that backwards, the result can be no better than how well he understood it. And that can be no better than how well he accepted it—and he can't accept anything until he gets confidence that he's going to be safe.

Ronnie observed that colts always feel safe around their mothers, who not only love and nurture them, but provide leadership—and yes, discipline when it's needed. Could it be that the mother horse is the ideal role model for a horseman?

Passive Predator

The biblical image of the lamb lying down with the lion emphasizes an important point about body language.

Horses communicate with each other using a language of gestures, from passive to aggressive. They also measure the threat that a predator poses by his body language. Best-selling trainer and author Monty Roberts offers an example of just how powerful that language is.

> The lions themselves, the preeminent predators on earth, they go passive too, and they lie on the side of the plain and they curl up their wrists and their claws and lie there relaxed, and the horses graze right by them—five, six feet from them—without worrying at all. It's when the cat's body says, "I'm now stalking" that the horse better get out of there.

So even though nature says you are a predator, you don't have to act like a predator. Mastering your own body language will dramatically improve your horsemanship.

Social Interaction

You may think you're a real party animal, but when it comes to socialization, horses have us beat by a mile.

Sure, most of us enjoy the company of other people, but we don't have the kind of deep-seated need for the herd that horses do. For horses in the wild, daily life revolves around socialization. Researcher Jaime Jackson elaborates:

> The activities—being around each other, playing, the foals playing, the meeting with other bands, with other horses, the whole social interaction that takes place—is very much part of what I call the teleology, their behavior complex. They need to be with each other. They thrive on each other's company, not only for reproduction, but for meeting their needs.

All horses do better when they can see and touch other horses. Unfortunately, the normal dominance games they play to establish their pecking order frighten some owners into isolating them.

Stallions Avoid Fighting

While it's true that stallions will fight with each other over a harem of mares, they usually try to avoid violence.

What is the real nature of the horse? In his quest to find out, equine photographer Robert Vavra observed and photographed horses in the wild. One of the most bizarre behaviors he documented was the dung ritual, a method stallions use to avoid a fight.

> You see the one stallion leaving his mare in estrus going over to the other stallion, who's approached him and been stalking him. The subordinate stallion dungs, and the other stallion dungs as the subordinate returns to his mares, and that way, that's their only confrontation. There's no physical fighting. In the rare occasion when neither one wants to show subordinance, there's parallel defecation.

This is a good example of just how different horses and humans are, and why communication between our species is sometimes challenging.

Everything Means Something

What separates master horse trainers from beginners? The masters understand every little gesture a horse makes. Modern horsemanship relies heavily on reinforcing desired behaviors from a horse. Sometimes the behavior you're after is simply an attitude shift, and the signs can be very subtle. In the 1980s, the late Montana horseman Ronnie Willis taught this important lesson to a young rodeo cowboy from California.

I think one of the things that maybe I was somewhat responsible for was that he began to notice the little things about the horse that made a big difference to the horse. See, nothing means nothing, but everything means something to that horse. And it's being able to recognize the slightest try, the smallest change that horse makes.

It was a lesson well learned, one that became integral to a horsemanship system now taught around the world by that California cowboy, Pat Parelli.

Predator Thinking

Maybe the most important thing to understand about horses is that they are prey animals and we are predators.

In nature's master plan, herbivores like deer, rabbits, and horses are prey animals, and they have an indirect way of getting things done. Carnivores like mountain lions, wolves, and humans are predators, and they're very direct in their actions. Australian trainer Clinton Anderson offers this example:

> A predator sees something it wants and it goes for it. We walk straight over and pick up the bucket. A horse will circle around it, look at it, smell it, investigate it, ponder on it, choose the best way to go up to it, and then have a back-out plan if the bucket goes to bite him.

Horses know we're predators, but they're willing to give us a chance if we don't act like predators. That's why the best horsemen seem to have a relaxed, roundabout way of approaching any task with a horse.

Why Horses Bite

Biting is one of the most dangerous things a horse can do to a human. But horses are selective about who they bite.

It's clearly an act of aggression when a horse bites, but how does he choose his victim? In a herd, a horse will not bite every other horse. And why would he bite you, but not me? Trainer GaWaNi Pony Boy offers this explanation.

Your status is the problem, the symptom being that you get bit. Does any horse in the herd, besides maybe an infant, ever dream about walking up to the alpha mare and taking a chunk out of her? They're just not crazy enough to do it. If you become the alpha, you never get bit.

Okay—so how do you become the alpha? By controlling your horse's movement—either causing him to move in a particular way or inhibiting his movement. This is what horses understand, and this is what most groundwork is all about.

Colts and Fillies

Nature has programmed horses to survive, so it's no wonder they have a healthy interest in the opposite sex.

According to the theme song of a popular sixties sitcom, "A horse is a horse," and when they're young, there's no appreciable difference between fillies and colts. They act about the same, you treat them about the same, and they don't seem to notice any difference themselves. Then, nature begins to takes its course. Native American clinician GaWaNi Pony Boy explains:

> At eleven to thirteen months, gender really becomes a factor. That's when a filly and a colt will start acting differently towards each other. Up until then, they're just babies; they start to recognize the difference around a year old.

Most experts recommend gelding (castrating) male horses not of breeding quality shortly after birth. Curiously, geldings may still show stallion-like interest in the opposite sex later in life, even though they can't do anything about it.

🐎 Mare Trains Foal

Want to learn the most effective way to train horses? Watch how a mare trains her foal and do the same.

Mother Nature has programmed the mare to begin teaching her baby how to be a horse from its first day of life. Clinician Pat Parelli has built the foal-training procedures of Parelli Natural Horsemanship on the same principles.

By the time we go to bed, go to work, do this, do that, a couple weeks go by. That mare and foal have got a lot of things going, and that's what we don't realize. The mare's the best trainer in the world. So I started not watching what people do but what the mare does. And I started getting more and more imagination, concepts on the kinds of things that I could get the foal to do with bombproofing, bonding, and then synchronization—getting them to follow and get into step and doing stuff like that. And they just pick it up so quickly.

Parelli developed his foal-training methods by combining his own observations with the imprint training regimen created by Dr. Robert M. Miller, one of his mentors.

Wanting to Lead

On trail rides, some horses seem intent on being at the front of the group, no matter what. Here's why.

In nature, horses seldom form a group and take off together unless a predator is chasing them. In the horse's mind, a trail ride fits that scenario. Add in the fact that the horses are usually strangers to one another, and you have the makings of a power struggle for lead position. Trainer Clinton Anderson explains:

> Some horses more than others say, "Okay, boys, I'm the leader. I don't know who you other guys are—we only met this morning—but I'm pretty good at being the leader. I'm going to be up front." Then your horse says, "Sorry, buddy. I don't know where you came from, but I'm the leader." And everybody's horse says, "Hey! *I'm* the leader." So now you've got seven horses that are all trying to lead a group of horses trying to run away from the imaginary tigers.

To convince your horse he's better off in the middle of the pack, put him to work when he surges to the front and let him rest at the desired position.

Horses Can't Get Along

Horses are herd animals and that's where they thrive. But just like kids, they do tend to fight at times.

Any time you have two or more horses together, they will decide which of them is the dominant or alpha horse. Some alpha horses are actually aggressive toward lesser members of the herd, which presents the owners with a dilemma, as described by trainer GaWaNi Pony Boy.

> If you're going to introduce a horse into a space where there's a very aggressive horse, you've got two choices. Your first choice is to remove the horseshoes from the horses and let them fight it out. Your second choice is to keep them separated for the rest of their lives. If I saw a major advantage—if I saw that one horse was definitely going to beat up another—I'd keep them separated. If I spent a lot of money on one horse, I'd keep them separated.

But generally speaking, Pony prefers letting horses work out their differences themselves. That, after all, is part of being a horse.

A Mare's Hormones

Never underestimate the power of hormones in the mother horse. They can turn her into a whole different animal.

You know that sweet little mare of yours? Once she has a baby, watch out! In an instant, she can turn vicious if she believes her foal needs protecting. It's all due to hormones, as veteran horseman Pat Parelli explains:

> This is nature's way of giving her super powers to be a super defender—supermom. Sometimes people make assumptions even with gentle horses. And at the same time, I've seen wild mares; the placental fluids get on you, and the smell of it, and they'll accept you. I've seen the darnedest things happen. That's why it's hard to give people just pat answers. Because you can't just say, "Oh, do this." Or, "Wild ones don't do that." Or, "Gentle ones are okay." It all depends.

Foals should be handled immediately after birth, with the mare present. Learning how to do this safely is part of your preparation for the big day.

 Context Shifts

When anything is taken out of its normal context, it can seem foreign and even threatening, to humans and horses alike.

Sound bites pulled out of speeches, faces seen in different surroundings, familiar sounds heard when we don't expect them—these are all examples of times when a shift in context changes the meaning we attach to sensory input. Horses go through the same thing. Five-star Parelli instructor David Lichman offers this example.

> Have you ever ridden your horse by the same raincoat hanging on the fence every single day, and one day somebody moved it one fence post over and you got bucked off? Horses are very sensitive to these context shifts.

And for good reason. The perceptivity of the horse to changes in its environment, and its ability to take flight instantaneously when frightened by those changes, are two reasons the horse has survived in its modern form for more than a million years.

Horse Mirrors Rider

There's a saying among computer programmers: Garbage in, garbage out. The same thing applies to horse training.

We all do it. We look outside of ourselves for the answers to our problems. But when we don't get what we want, from either a computer or a horse, it's more often due to bad programming than to faulty processing. Horseman Tom Nagel is a black-belt martial artist and Zen priest. He advises that we look at the horse's behavior as a reflection of ourselves and what we are doing right or wrong.

> There's definitely differences in horses, and horses have their own personalities. Some horses serve as a better mirror than others. But what I'm finding is that every horse, at some point, can serve almost as a teacher for you, as a mirror to reflect back what you're doing.

Most problems arise from inconsistency or lack of clarity in our communication with the horse, and can be resolved by turning up our own self-discipline.

Memories and Categories

Horses, like most animals, have mental processes quite different from those of humans—at least, most humans. Dr. Temple Grandin of Colorado State University is one of the world's leading experts on autism because she has it and, remarkably, can talk about it. She draws parallels between the mental processes of animals and those of autistic humans.

Animals are going to think in sensory-based memories: visual memories, smell memories, touch memories, auditory memories. And then to form a concept, they have to put those together in categories and associate them. And that's exactly the same way that I think. And there are some philosophers that say, "Well, if you don't have language, you can't possibly be conscious or think." Well, then I would have to conclude that I'm not able to think.

Grandin has developed language as a way of narrating the images in her head, and that has enabled her to offer new insights into the workings of the animal mind.

Genderless Horse

Are you sexist when it comes to horses? Many people are! They prejudge a horse based on its gender.

The women's movement in America fostered the idea that no one should be stereotyped by his or her sex. That's a good rule of thumb for horses, too. Clinician Dan Sumerel elaborates:

> I walk up to a horse and I treat him as a horse or treat her as a horse, because first and foremost, a horse is a horse. Secondarily, it is a male or female, and thirdly, it is a particular breed or age. If I can influence that horse's mind and get his attitude to come around—if his mind agrees to go with me—his genitals will follow.

Yes, stallions can be dangerous, but so can mares and geldings. The fact is, most equine behavior is not driven by gender. It's driven by the dominance games all horses play with one another and with us to determine who's going to be leader.

Normal Patterns

No matter how foreign the equine mind may seem to us humans, one simple fact makes training it possible.

Colorado horseman John Lyons is one of America's most popular teachers of horsemanship. He explains why it is possible for us to train a species so very different from our own.

Horses do normal things for horses. For example, they don't chase down lions, kill them, and eat them. And so, because they live within a certain pattern of behavior, that allows us to know what's going to happen, how the horse is going to respond. Basically, there should be no surprises.

Of course, we do need to educate ourselves about how a horse thinks and lives before we can know what constitutes his normal behavior. Fortunately, the horse industry is one of America's largest, and it is brimming with resources to help us understand the horse and successfully develop a relationship with him.

The Play Drive

Just like you and me, horses have their priorities in life, but
they're completely different than ours.

Horses are at their most free and most athletic when playing with one another. But around humans, horses tend to be
preoccupied with issues more basic than play. Natural horseman Pat Parelli offers this example:

> It's their instinct to be safe, to be comfortable, and then
> when everything's fine, to play. You never see horses stop
> and say, "Time out, lions. We want to play right now." They
> don't play when they feel threatened. They only play when
> everything feels great to them.

As far as horses are concerned, humans are like lions—
we're predators—but as we grow in our horsemanship, we
learn how to not act like predators. That's central to Parelli
Natural Horsemanship, a system that leads to a sort of uncon-
scious competence, or what Pat calls *savvy*, and savvy is the key
that unlocks the play drive in any horse.

Natural Horsemanship

You've probably heard the term bandied about, but what exactly *is* natural horsemanship?

The book (and later, film), *The Horse Whisperer*, by Nicholas Evans, brought the idea of natural horsemanship to the masses, but left many with a rather simplistic view of what it means. Australian clinician Clinton Anderson:

> Sometimes people have a little bit different concept of natural horsemanship—that it's just a bunch of whispering and patting and stuff like that. I think to really define it, natural horsemanship is just looking at things from the horse's point of view. Horses scratch each other and rub each other all the time, but they also bite and kick and squeal. You've got to be able to look at both sides of the scale.

It's all about communicating with a horse in ways that are natural to him, not to us. This means becoming masters of our own body language, something many humans don't know much about—that is, unless they're poker players or car salesmen.

Sitting Horse

You sometimes see a horse sitting on his haunches as part of an entertainment act, but sitting is actually a useful exercise.

Sitting down, then standing up repeatedly in a controlled manner, is difficult for most horses, but it helps relax and condition the horse's back. Trainer J.P. Giacomini describes how this unusual exercise helped one tall, long-backed warmblood horse.

> That horse's canter totally changed. It came from a very discombobulated canter that was going too fast, giving his rider an enormous amount of problems, to a very collected canter with depart from the walk—looked like a little Western lope—and this horse couldn't have done that with a year of dressage training if we hadn't done the exercise.

On their own, horses will sit for a moment while getting to their feet after rolling in the dirt or napping in the sun. Sometimes you'll even see them rotate a bit while seated, either to itch their behinds or stretch their backs.

Horses vs. Kids

For anyone who has kids, the principles of horse training will probably seem kind of familiar.

While it's true that humans and equines are very different species, parents will quickly realize that training horses is a lot like raising kids. Trainer Clinton Anderson explains:

> Horses and children are so much the same it's incredible, because children will test you. A lot of them know what right and wrong is, but they will always try and test that wrong avenue if they get a chance. They have an abundance of energy, but if you don't channel that energy in the right direction, they start getting in trouble. Horses are exactly the same. If you don't give them something to do, I guarantee *they're* going to give *you* something to do, and whatever they make you do ain't gonna be half as fun as what you could have made them do.

Children and horses feel safer when they know you're in charge and that there are boundaries to acceptable behavior. Done correctly, a reprimand reinforces your leadership position and makes both of you feel more secure.

Early Learning

Horses can be trained at any age, but unlike many species, horses learn fastest in their first week of life.

Every species has periods in its development when it's programmed to learn the most efficiently. Some need this very early in life in order to survive; the horse, for example. Dr. Robert M. Miller, creator of imprint training, explains:

> The horse, unlike human babies or puppies or kittens, is a precocial creature; born with a completely mature brain and all senses functioning, its learning ability is at its peak in those first few days of life. What happens early in life is permanently impressed into that brain.

It only makes sense, then, to capitalize on this weeklong super-learning period by teaching the foal as much as possible. Obviously, you can't ride him, but you can teach him other things he'll need later in life, like accepting being handled, leading and tying, and moving away from pressure.

Foal Gentles Mare

We know that foals learn much about life from their mothers, but what can mares learn from their foals?

One of the cutest things you'll ever see is a young foal emulating its mother, going where she goes, trying to eat what she eats, acting like she acts. But as natural horsemanship guru Pat Parelli relates, this can have a positive effect on the mare as well, especially when an early training regimen is followed with the foal.

> I've got a mare that I've had for years that's a real skeptic, and she's always been hard to catch and all this. Well, we found that since we started the foal imprinting program and the early learning, we keep the mare and the foal for the first thirty days up in the yard. The foal gets so gentle that it just keeps dragging the mare up near us. Now she's getting to where she's less of a skeptic herself, so it's almost kind of reversed itself.

This gives new hope to breeders who might have been reluctant to breed an otherwise good mare because she had a difficult temperament.

Suspicious Horse

Every horse is suspicious, to a greater or lesser degree, of who and what is around him.

French horse trainer J.P. Giacomini has studied the learning process in horses and has concluded that, although it's a natural part of the horse's survival mechanism, suspicion interferes with learning.

> The normal horse has to be suspicious and cannot wait to find out if he's right or wrong, because then it's usually too late. So he just leaves the scene or prepares himself to do one of his natural defenses—kick, strike, bite, whatever. While he's doing this, he won't be able to get any information from us that will teach him a new process, because this learning would require his attention and relaxation.

Conversely, if we can induce relaxation in the horse, we'll facilitate learning. J.P. relaxes a horse by rhythmically tapping him with what he calls an Endo-Stick. This procedure is called Endo-Tapping.

Mare with Foal

Everyone knows that a mare can be a little, shall we say, crabby? It often gets worse when she has a foal at her side. A mother mare instinctively feels protective about her foal. Even when she's not worried about you hurting Junior, she may still act annoyed if you show him a lot of attention. Why would that be? That's right: jealousy! Clinician GaWaNi Pony Boy explains:

I've found that when you have a mare with a foal by her side, if you treat the mare as if the foal were not there—just focus on the mare, and don't pay any attention to the foal—you'll usually do just fine. It's when you start focusing on the foal that she starts to notice you're paying more attention to her baby, and you start to have some difficulties.

Not all mares react this way. In fact, when imprint training is practiced with a newborn foal, the mare is more likely to treat the handler as part of the family. She'll accept the handling and training of her baby with a ho-hum kind of attitude.

Flight as Primary Defense

Among domestic animals, horses are unique in their primary means of defending themselves: They simply run away.

Understanding the importance of the flight instinct in the horse is key to understanding the horse himself. When he feels his safety is threatened, the horse's first inclination is to get out of town. Equine behaviorist Dr. Robert M. Miller describes this instinct:

> Creatures have several defenses, including a primary defense and a secondary defense. In the case of the horse, their secondary defense would be to strike or kick or bite—but the primary defense is to run away. This is not true of wild cattle, wild sheep, or wild goats; they have their horns to protect them, as wild dogs have teeth. But the horse is a flight creature. It's the only domestic animal that uses flight as a primary defense in the wild state.

But doesn't domestication change this? In a word, no. To quote Mr. Ed, "A horse is a horse . . . of course, of course."

A Horse's Reaction Time

Flight first, fight second. That's the priority system of a horse whose survival instinct has kicked in.

When you confine a horse, you eliminate his primary defense mechanism—running away—so when he feels threatened, nature has programmed him to go to a second line of defense: striking back. As veterinarian and horse trainer Robert M. Miller explains, the reaction time of the horse is the fastest of any domestic animal, and you're no match for that.

> It's like the strike of a rattlesnake. Even an old, decrepit horse can move with such speed that if a horse wants to strike you or kick you, not to intimidate you but to really get you, you will not be able to avoid it. I don't care how young and athletic you are.

Dr. Miller teaches ways of handling a horse that minimize your vulnerability to kicking and biting through body positioning, leverage on the head and feet, and keeping the horse calm. He calls it defensive horsemanship.

🐴 Loyal Mare

Like men and women, male and female horses differ in how they approach relationships.

Dr. John Gray has taught us that *Men Are from Mars, Women Are from Venus.* In other words, there are real differences in the way the sexes think. Accepting that fact is the first step to improving male/female relationships. Likewise, you need to understand how mares differ from male horses, as clinician GaWaNi Pony Boy explains:

> Mares, if you put the time into them, are willing to give you just total commitment. But if you're not willing to give them that time, they could just care less who you are. I've found that alpha mares tend to be easier once you break through that front. You get these guys who spend eight, ten hours on their mare's back and they develop a real relationship. And then you've got a tremendously loyal mare that will just die for the guy.

It's not unusual for a hard-riding cowboy to prefer the fairer sex for his equine partner.

CHAPTER TWO

Training

Knowledge in Disguise

Do you think you lack the patience necessary to train a horse?
Don't despair. It may not take as much as you think.

Good horsemen will persist with a horse through seem-
ingly endless repetitions of an exercise before getting the result
they're after. What keeps them going when others would give
up? Are horsemen just exceptionally patient people? Clinician
John Lyons offers this encouragement:

> You don't need patience to train a horse. It's the most
> overrated commodity. Knowledge looks like patience in
> disguise. The only reason we ever get discouraged is
> because we don't think we're getting anywhere. The rea-
> son we don't think we're getting anywhere is because
> sometimes when we actually *are* getting somewhere, we
> don't look "small" enough to see this horse is on the right
> track. He's going to make it.

A horse goes through a predictable series of responses
when learning something. Some are very subtle, but the
trained eye sees each little improvement.

Magnetized Horse

Horses often have a strong desire to be at a particular place or with another horse, almost like they're magnetized. If a horse doesn't want to leave the barn, he's called barn sour. If he doesn't want to leave his companions in the herd, he's called herd bound or buddy sour. But *sour* in this case doesn't mean ruined, as popular Aussie horse trainer and clinician Clinton Anderson explains.

Horses have what you call magnets. They're always magnetized toward something: the barn, the other horse, the horse in the paddock, whatever it is. Let them go to whatever is drawing them. And when you find that, just keep their feet moving and then let them rest wherever the magnet isn't. Pretty soon, the horse doesn't want to go near what he thought he wanted to go near.

Horses are basically lazy creatures. They quickly figure out what situations mean more work or discomfort for them, and those are the situations they want to avoid.

Intimidation in Training

You can intimidate a horse into performing a certain way, but you'll be making more work for yourself in the long run.

Let's set aside any questions about the morality of harsh horse-training methods. They do work, and they've worked for centuries. The problem is, they have little staying power compared to gentle methods. Trainer Mike Kevil asks us to consider what happens when you give horses trained with each approach a couple months off.

> That is where you'll see the difference. You'll get on the horse that has been intimidated and you're going to have to intimidate him all over again. You see, he knows what's coming—the big, strong punch and the spur—and he's ready to fight you. The other horse, because he learned in a soft way, and you ended that way, he trusts you. When you get on, he just goes right on with the program.

So, the fact of the matter is, the gentle methods of natural horsemanship are not only morally superior—they actually work better.

Anger, Fear, Impatience

There are three human emotions most of us feel every day that will sabotage communication with a horse.

It's normal to feel angry when a horse misbehaves, afraid when you think you're in danger, or impatient when training takes longer than expected. But in every case, responding emotionally makes the situation worse. Since we can't simply turn off our emotions, Dr. Robert M. Miller offers this suggestion.

We have to discipline ourselves for when this occurs—not if, because it *will* occur—we're human beings; we're going to get angry sometimes, we're going to be afraid sometimes, and we're going to be impatient sometimes. And what you do is stop right there and walk away from that horse, because you have lost the ability to communicate with a horse when you are impatient or angry or afraid.

Walking away may require swallowing your pride—but that's one more emotion you can't allow to rule you.

Training All the Time

How often should you train your horse? The best horsemen are training all the time.

There are many chances to interact with your horse that may not seem like training opportunities. In fact, training may be the furthest thing from your mind. But your horse doesn't know that. Every contact you have with him tells him about your fitness to lead and what you expect of him. Oregon author, judge, clinician, and trainer Richard Shrake elaborates:

> The really great horseman, whether he's dressage, cutting, or whatever, he's constantly training his horse every time he gets on him. He'll move his shoulder; he'll back him up. When he saddles him, he'll side-pass him over to put the saddle up. When he gets ready to put him in the trailer, he'll back him up that one step and then load him. The good ones realize that it's so important to be doing this type of training all the time.

Horses respond best to consistency in our behavior, and that's what this is all about.

Ending on a Good Note

When it comes to practicing just about anything, they say it's best to end on a good note. But sometimes you can't.

If it were a perfect world, you would know exactly when to end every training session: right when your horse was at his very best. But it's not a perfect world, and there's no way for you to know that. So just relax. When things start going downhill, it's often time to call it a day. Dressage instructor and author Mike Schaffer shares this insight:

> Never once in my whole life have I gotten off a horse and said, "Darn, I wish I'd stayed on for another two minutes. Something great would have happened." But there have been dozens of times when I've just stayed on for two minutes too long and really taken what would've been a wonderful ride and managed to mess it up.

If you find yourself wondering if your horse has had enough, he probably has. Listen to that inner voice of yours, and remember—there's always tomorrow.

Teaching Both Sides

It's a trap into which we humans sometimes fall: assuming horses learn the same way we do.

If you learn to do something with your left hand, you understand how to do it with your right hand as well. You may not be as coordinated or have as much strength, but your brain has all the programming needed for the crossover. Horses are different. A horse's left and right sides may be inches apart on his body but worlds apart in his brain, according to trainer Vaughn Knudsen.

> In people, we can reason through it, so what our left hand knows it can teach the right hand. A horse does not have that ability because the nerve endings do not cross over; they just can't process and teach both sides.

This is why much of horse gentling and training is devoted to what seems like redundant activity: working both sides evenly. But in one sense, horses and humans are similar. Each of us tends to be better on one side than the other.

Expanding the Comfort Zone

Do you want a horse that's easily upset by what goes on around him? Or would you rather have one that takes it in stride? Trainer Clinton Anderson defines three zones in the horse's mind. In the comfort zone, the horse is relaxed and confident. In the unsure zone, he's nervous and concerned. And in the life-threatening zone, he's having an all-out panic attack. We want to expand the horse's comfort zone, and the only way to do that, Clinton says, is to cause him to venture outside of it.

Every time you push your horse into the unsure zone, and then you don't let him return until he learns something, that comfort zone gets bigger and bigger. Basically, he learns to tolerate more and more things. He also learns to be sensitized and move away from more sources of pressure.

The horse tells you he's learned something by softening his eye, lowering his head, and licking his lips. These signs indicate that you can remove the stimulus that initially made him unsure.

The Focus Game

The world is full of distractions for your horse. Getting him to focus on the task at hand starts with you.

You can't change what goes on around you and your horse, and sometimes you will lose his attention. Trainer John Lyons suggests that you have an exercise ready to work on, focus on doing that exercise, and be ready for a little mental battle with your horse.

> The horse is trying to play a game. I bet I can make you think of the buddy horse. *No, no, I'm doing this.* But I'm throwing my head over here. *No, no, I'm doing this.* But the fence is coming up. *No, no, I'm doing this.* But there's a lot of people. *No, no, I'm doing this.* And so, it's just a game, and it's learning how to keep our focus on that game. Then what's going to happen, the longer I stay focused, pretty soon that horse is going to come right over and start working on what I'm working on.

Avoid checking out the distraction yourself. It usually doesn't matter what it is, and if you let it draw your attention, you've lost the focus game.

Petting a Horse

Horses enjoy the loving touch of a human being, but there's a right way and a wrong way to pet your horse.

Horses are basically suspicious creatures at heart, and if we act unsure or tentative when we touch them, they're liable to think something's wrong. Veteran horseman Kenny Harlow explains how he pets a horse.

> I just go up and pet him. If you go and cup your hand, and turn it down, and do all that stuff and go nice and slow and let him sniff at you and all, the horse is going to think you're somewhat scared to start with. If you just walk up and pet him like he's a dead-broke, quiet horse, then that's what he's going to act like. If you act like he's dangerous, he's going to act dangerous.

Horses are not big dogs. They don't like to be patted or slapped, even though most will tolerate a certain amount of that. The best way to pet a horse is to stroke, rub, or gently scratch him, and until you get to know him, it's best to first pet him on his neck.

Longeing and Long-Lining

Conscientious trainers today use longeing and long-lining exercises to prepare horses for riding.

Sticklers for accuracy prefer the French spelling *longe* over the American *lunge*, but both refer to working a horse in a circle at the end of a line attached to his halter. Long-lining is similar, except the horse is in a bridle and bit, and the trainer works him using long reins. British trainer Tanya Larrigan explains the purpose of each exercise.

> With young horses, we do longeing. He then is developing the muscles over his back, so he's able to carry a rider when they get on. And the work you're doing with the reins, you're actually developing the mouth. And all this time, you're building up trust and cooperation with him.

Too many people longe a horse before riding simply to tire him out, when the real purpose should be to get him warmed up and paying attention.

Aiming of Your Belly Button

For greater success in working your horse in a round pen, become aware of where you're aiming your belly button. Imagine the place on a horse's body where the girth strap rides. Physical or psychological pressure applied in front of the girth line (or "drive" line) opposes the forward movement of the horse; pressure applied behind supports it. As Canadian clinician Chris Irwin explains, the place you are applying pressure is determined not by where you stand, but by your angle to the horse; in other words, where your belly button is aimed.

Physically, we might have our body located behind the girth of the horse, thinking we're tapping into the horse's herding impulse. But if when that horse looks at us, it sees that the belly button is aimed at the head, which nine times out of ten with people it is, that horse does not associate our movement with pushing. That horse associates our movement with capturing, which is a fundamentally different message.

Stages of Pressure

A horse won't ever mistake you for another horse, but he'll be more responsive if you act a little like one.

What horses understand intuitively is body language. The lead mare establishes her dominance in a herd through a series of gestures that escalate in intensity. Clinician Clinton Anderson explains.

> She's going to do whatever she can to get the job done. She's going to start out by just pinning her ears and putting a bit of a sour look on her face, and if every other horse moves out of her space, that's as far as it goes. If they don't, she's going to act like she's going to bite them. If they don't move then, she's going to bite them. If they still don't move, then she's going to act like she's going to kick them. If they still don't move, she's going to kick them. So she goes through a few different stages of pressure. She just doesn't walk in there and start kicking everybody.

In the herd or the training pen, idle threats don't work; you have to be willing to turn up the heat with your horse. Be consistent about it and you'll eventually have a horse that responds to the lightest of touches.

Training the Alpha Horse

In every group of horses, there is a leader or alpha horse. How do you deal with a horse that's used to being the boss? The dominant horse in the herd lives that role twenty-four hours a day. She must assert her leadership continually or she'll lose it. Now enter a human, who says "I'm in charge here." Conflict and resistance from the horse are inevitable. Clinician Richard Shrake says the best way to handle the alpha horse is to remain focused and always have an agenda when you work with her.

Now that doesn't mean to be cruel to her. It doesn't mean to be aggressive. It just means to take that leadership role and have a plan of doing something, whether it's moving her shoulders, backing her up, doing trail, doing reining maneuvers. But you've got to have an objective of being busy with her, training all the time.

The good news is that an alpha horse often has a strong work ethic and will try harder for you if you know how to ask.

Introducing Weight on the Horse's Back

It used to be called *breaking*. Today it's called *starting* a horse, but it still requires the horse to accept weight on its back.

The change in terminology is more than just political correctness. The goal today is not to break a horse's spirit, but to train his mind to accept human leadership. If the horse is destined to be a riding animal, there's also another hurdle to clear: getting him to tolerate something on his back. Instinct tells him to fight it, like he would fight a mountain lion. But by introducing weight gradually, we can overcome that fear reaction, according to trainer Sharon Smith.

> You start with a blanket; next day, put a saddle on. After that, tighten it up. Day after that, lean on him. It's a slow procedure to get him to accept weight on the back.

For the sake of demonstration, clinicians sometimes do the entire procedure in thirty minutes, but they'd be the first to tell you there's no reason to rush it.

Navajo Ring

It sounds like a page right out of a modern natural horseman-ship manual, but the Navajo ring is an old gentling method.

Trainer Frank Bell shares gentling techniques with other wild horse enthusiasts, like Tennessean Robert Demlinger, who taught him the Navajo ring, where twelve to fifteen people encircle a young horse, creating a gradually shrinking human round pen.

> You start to move in. The horse will come over and take a sniff, and maybe you'd be able to stroke it a little bit. Next thing you know, it's sniffing somebody else, and then somebody's stroking its rump. Apparently it's something that was really used by the Indians years and years ago, and it makes perfect sense. You don't put too much heat on them. You just let the horses get comfortable around the humans and find out that they can trust, that touch isn't a bad thing. Now we're starting to use a little pres-sure and release, and the whole thing progresses pretty fast.

Gentling wild horses is popular partly because the horse has no emotional baggage from previous contact with humans.

Clipper Training

When you're teaching a horse to accept electric clippers, don't plan on actually clipping him for a while.

Horses hate electric clippers, and it's not because they prefer that wild and woolly look. They're frightened by the sound and the vibration. So that's where trainer Clinton Anderson focuses his desensitization efforts.

> When I'm teaching a horse to accept clippers, the last thing I'm trying to do is clip him. See, it's a cat and mouse game. If a horse thinks you're trying to clip him, that's when he'll act the worst because he knows what you want. All I'm trying to do is get the horse used to the vibration of the clippers and the noise of the clippers. Once I get those two things established, the actual clipping of the hair usually is very, very simple.

Sound like a roundabout way to deal with the issue? It is! We're suppressing our straight-line, predator-type thinking and sneaking up on the problem, like a horse would.

Impersonating a Cow

In the training of a cow horse, it sometimes helps to start him working other animals, like horses, or even humans. Paul Dietz is an Arizona horseman who specializes in teaching horses and people to work with cattle. In his clinics, he has found that young horses often need to practice their moves on something slower and less agile than a cow.

Sometimes we might get people working each other's horses. In other words, you've got two riders, and one rider might be playing the cow and get the horse to hook onto the other horse where he can make the turns and block the horse. Or we might get somebody afoot just working on getting them to hook onto somebody afoot where you can block the person. This can be a valuable exercise, because the person can be a little more forgiving than the cow sometimes, and help the younger horse.

Other trainers incorporate mechanical cows that can be turned and run one direction or the other using remote controls.

The Replacement Concept

Horses sometimes do things we don't like, but there's a positive way of saying no to them.

John Lyons is one of America's most popular teachers of horsemanship. One of his most ingenious training ideas is called the replacement concept. John puts the horse to work on an unrelated positive task when he exhibits negative behavior.

> For an example, he may be biting. I may work on softening his shoulders, moving his hips, picking up leads. What happens is, he starts doing more and more of what I do want and less and less of what I don't want. Pretty soon, what I don't want is nonexistent, and I've never even brought the subject up to him. I've never said to him, "Don't bite."

There's an important principle here: A horse can't be thinking about two things at the same time. Keep him busy doing one thing and he soon has to give it 100 percent of his attention. John's pet name for this principle? The "walk and chew gum theory."

Assertive, Nonthreatening Leader

A partner or a leader. What is the better role for you to play
with your horse? The ideal has elements of both.

Every serious horseman is searching for the same thing in
his relationship with his horse: the respect afforded a leader
and the trust afforded a partner. Canadian clinician, equine
behaviorist, and corporate trainer Chris Irwin puts it this way:

> When we're working with the horse, we're trying to estab-
> lish ourselves as an assertive but nonthreatening leader,
> to find that perfect bond with your horse where you are
> the one leading the dance, but it's not forced. It's not
> coerced. You've truly developed a willing partnership with
> the horse.

Taken to the workplace, this is a good model for an effective manager—someone who has the assertiveness to lead con-
vincingly without threat or intimidation, and with empathy for
those he leads. How many bosses like that have you had?

Rhythm and Desensitization

A proven technique for dealing with a horse's fear is to present the scary object repeatedly, with rhythm.

Aussie clinician Clinton Anderson is a master at solving problems with horses. He explains how a horse's brain processes things that scare him in nature.

> When something spooks a horse, usually the horse jumps and gets frightened because he thinks it's going to hurt him. And then the stimulus stops. The dogs stop barking, the car's passed you, the plastic bag flew across in front you. And the horse says, "I know how I got rid of that; I acted like a prey animal, got scared, and this thing disappeared.

However, when a stimulus is presented over and over, with rhythm, the horse eventually realizes that spooking hasn't made it go away, and as long as it's not hurting him, he'll begin to relax. Scientists call this *habituation*, and we experience it, too. Like the way we tune out the ticking of a clock.

⬤ Facing Fear

You can't eliminate fear in a horse, and you shouldn't try. Instead, teach him to face what scares him.

Horses are born "fraidy cats," and nature has programmed them to take flight when frightened. The first step to reprogramming the fear response is to accept that fear is normal and even useful for a horse. Trainer GaWaNi Pony Boy explains:

> If you're a horse and you're walking on a cliff, it's good to have fear; it's good to be afraid of mountain lions, and it's good to be afraid of semi trucks. What you do with that fear is another matter. Now, it's their natural instinct to go up in the air, spin around, and run away. We want to try to train them to face that fear. Turn and look at what you're afraid of.

The turning and facing maneuver requires some rational thought; it positions the horse so it's harder to bolt and run; and it gives him a chance to look at the scary object. Often this simple movement is enough to eliminate the impulse to "get outta Dodge."

Working a Cow in a Round Pen

Some cow horses are born and some are made, but they both benefit from some time in the round pen.

Round pen training is usually ground training; in other words, the rider is not mounted on the horse. But cow horse trainer Paul Dietz has found the fifty- to sixty-foot round pen to be a good place to give a cow horse his first real chance at working a cow with a rider on his back.

> With the round pen, I can put the cow where he's on the outside; when the cow turns, rather than the cow outrunning me if he runs a little faster, I can cut across the round pen and cut off the distance. This is because the cow on the outside of the round pen has to make quite a bit more tracks than my horse. So if my horse is a little late, I've found that I don't have to get after him quite so much.

This offers the horse more time to actually work the cow, rather than chase it. Few horses need practice at that.

The Horse Slows Down

There are some techniques used in horse training that are completely counterintuitive to us humans. For instance, any horse will eventually slow down if you ride him long enough. How do you prevent that? *Ask* him to slow down! Trainer John Lyons explains:

> If we think he's going to slow down when we get to twenty feet, we actually want to pick up on the reins and slow him down at eighteen feet. So, just before you think your horse is going to slow down on his own, you ask him to slow down. And then pretty soon he waits longer and longer for you to tell him so you can ride him farther at the speed that you want.

Trickery? Reverse psychology? You bet! But it works, and teaching a horse to maintain his state of motion until further notice is one of a trainer's most important jobs.

 **Red Light**

Just as we sometimes wake up on the wrong side of the bed, a horse can wake up on the wrong side of the stall.

An important thing to realize about horses is that they are subject to moods just like we are. A horse can be happy and ready to learn, or grumpy and resistant to learning. Trainer Richard Shrake describes how to tell the difference:

> A red light—when he's saying, "I'm not going to handle this anymore; it's way beyond my pressure point"—will be a tightness. He's tight in his eyes, tight in his nostrils, he has a busy tail. When he's just stiff, or he just stops; when he raises his head up and his ears are back, a real chomp and a drop of the head, and pulling the reins out of the hand. These signals are pretty easy to see.

If you're getting red lights from your horse, it's best not to force the issue. The window of opportunity for training simply isn't open at that moment. Instead, do something simpler that you know your horse will tolerate.

🐴 Green Light

When is your horse in the right frame of mind to learn? He'll tell you, but you have to understand his language.

When two horses confront one another in a herd environment, the more submissive horse indicates that through his body language. He shows that he is tuned in to the other horse and accepts his leadership. These are the same kinds of signals we look for in a training session. Clinician Richard Shrake calls them green lights.

The green light—when he says, "I'm hooked, I'm listening"—that learning window is open. You'll see a lick and a chew. You'll see a deep breath, a relaxation. You'll see the horse soft and supple when you pick up the rein. He breaks in the poll. He gives you his face. His legs slow down, you know, and man, that's when it's good.

If this sounds like a relaxed and comfortable horse, it is! Remember, horses must have a leader, and they are happiest when you show them you're competent and confident in that role.

A Rearing Horse

If a movie horse rears for the camera, it's a stunt. If your horse rears when you longe him, it's just dangerous.

To cure a horse of rearing, trainer Clinton Anderson uses a rope halter and a fourteen-foot lead rope. He stands back and urges the horse to longe or circle him to the left by pointing the lead rope high in the air with his left hand and twirling the free end of the rope with his right hand. Clinton says it's important not to stop when the horse rears.

> Your horse may jump in the air ten, fifteen times, and you're back far enough where you're not in any danger of him rearing up on top of you; you're not standing under his nose. You're just twirling, and if he rears up twenty times, you just sit there and keep twirling. But the second he moves off to the left, you quit twirling, and that's his reward.

Rearing requires a great deal of exertion for a horse, so eventually he'll tire and stop. Next time he feels like rearing, he'll remember how little he gained from all that effort.

Patience and Knowledge

There are two things you need in abundance if you want to be a good horseman: patience and knowledge.

Have you ever noticed that the best horsemen are both calm and confident? These are outward signs of patience and knowledge. Patience is manifested in a calm demeanor, a willingness to give the horse time to work things out. A strong base of knowledge gives the horseman the confidence he needs to be a leader to the horse. As trainer Mike Schaffer points out, there's an interesting correlation between patience and knowledge.

The rider's patience and knowledge run out at the same time. Once you know that, the next time you find yourself losing your patience with a horse, there's a little voice going off in the back of your head saying, "You know what? You're just frustrated because you don't know what to do with this."

Remember the old rule about counting to ten before losing your temper? With a horse, you may need to count a little further to regain your patience and to access your knowledge.

Three Points of Contact

To avoid injury with horses, there are only two safe places to be: far away, or in close contact.

Accidents often occur when horses are startled and their self-preservation instincts kick in. Renowned equine behaviorist Dr. Robert M. Miller explains why closer contact makes this less likely to happen.

> In most of the things we do with horses, the horse really can't see you. He's looking at you with one eye, and he's looking at you with his peripheral vision out of the corner of the eye. So if you're in body contact with him, you're communicating with that horse in a second way. He feels your contact.

Dr. Miller recommends a minimum of three points of contact when working with a horse from the ground. In addition to using both hands, he often presses his hip or elbow against the horse. This has a calming effect, and the three points form a triangle, giving the handler a certain architectural advantage he wouldn't otherwise have.

Abuse Excuse

You've just bought a new horse and you find out he was abused by the previous owner. What do you do?

What one person sees as a legitimate training technique, someone else may see as abusing a horse, so even defining abuse becomes problematic. Trainer Clinton Anderson often encounters what you might call the abuse excuse.

When you take all this emotional baggage with you to the arena, every time your horse does something silly or something you don't want, you say, "Ah, well, he's got a good reason to act like that because he was abused." So when I get an owner like that, I say, "Hey, you're in luck! You just bought the horse from me today. You don't know any history. You don't know anything about it. Start moving on." And as soon as the owner treats it like that, you'd be amazed at the improvement they make.

Think about how horses treat each other. If a new horse joins the herd, the other horses expect him to behave appropriately *today*. They really don't care what happened before.

Freshening a Horse

If you spend most of your riding time in an arena practicing show maneuvers, you will eventually have a sour horse.

Horses are remarkably compliant to our wishes, but you can tell when they're not too happy about it. Richard Shrake is a respected clinician, judge, and trainer of Western show horses. He feels horses need work with a real purpose to keep them mentally fit.

> I never, never saw a horse that had a job to do really get sour. Out riding in the open, gathering cattle, he's always got a job to do. He's happy. But today when we have our arena horses, our pleasure horses that we kind of ride in circles, going around and around—they get bored.

To freshen up the bored horse, Richard recommends using poles, cones, and other obstacles to create a course that will challenge his mind and his body. It may not be the same as chasing cattle across a mountain meadow, but it's a start.

Working through Doubt

There are times when we must forge ahead with a task even if we're not sure it's the right course of action. But not always.

Working through doubt to a successful outcome can be an empowering life experience. But as clinician John Lyons illustrates, doubt is sometimes a red flag, a subconscious signal that we need to slow down and reconsider how we're doing things.

> If you're working a horse and just the thought passes in front of your eyes, the horse might be working too hard, he might be getting too hot, you want to quit right then. You can't ever get hurt with a horse by quitting too early, but you can get hurt with a horse by quitting too late.

Working with horses, you develop an intuition, an instinct about what they are telling you through their body language. It's really just another form of knowledge, but one that humans often don't use. Listening to and trusting that inner voice is important in becoming a horseman.

Never the Horse's Fault

Set your fragile human ego up on the shelf. When you have a problem with your horse, it's usually your fault.

Does your horse want you to fail? When things aren't going right, it's easy to think so. But a horse doesn't have the mental capacity to be devious or malicious, to deliberately thwart you in reaching your goals. Dressage instructor Mike Schaffer elaborates:

> Most of the time, what I see when I'm working with students and they're frustrated or they have a problem with the horse, what they don't realize—and I come in as the third party and stand there and look objectively—is that the horse is doing exactly what they're asking him to do. We've seen a few horses who eventually just give up on us humans and they say, "You know what? You people are just too difficult. I can't deal with you." They really don't want to play with us anymore, and that's unfortunate.

Horses are only capable of being horses, and you'll be a better horseman if you let this rule guide you: It's never the horse's fault.

🐎 Cinchy Horse

If your horse gets upset when you tighten the girth strap, don't worry. Here's a solution that's so easy, it's a cinch.

When you remember that a horse is naturally claustrophobic, it's easy to understand why the constriction of a cinch or girth strap around the middle can set him off. Clinician Clinton Anderson offers this technique for desensitizing the girth area.

> I wouldn't tie him up. I wouldn't even worry about the saddle. I'd get the end of the lead rope, I'd throw it over his back, right where the girth would be, and I'd pick it up like it's a girth. And I'd pull both ends of the lead rope up so it squeezes on his belly. And he'll probably get a little toey and a little antsy, and he'll move around a little bit. Just let him move around, and then when he stops moving his feet, drop it and relax it. Rub him. Go do it again.

This is a good example of the correlation that so much of horse training tries to create in the horse's mind: Whenever I get upset, things will get better if I stop moving my feet and just relax.

Cold to the Feel

Combine a severe bit with heavy hands and chances are, your horse will become "cold to the feel."

The goal of every horseman is to have a horse that responds instantly to the subtlest of cues. The more severe the bit, the subtler that cue can become because the horse feels the slightest movement of the rider's hands. Ironically, handling a horse roughly while he's wearing such a bit can have exactly the opposite effect, as show horse trainer Richard Shrake explains.

> When that bit's too severe, he kind of tightens his jaw, tightens his shoulder, and kind of goes, "Whoop! Don't do that again!" And when he does that, he's desensitized and he's cold to the feel. So, what happens sometimes, you do this enough to a horse, and pretty soon he just doesn't listen.

A horse can also learn to grab the bit with his teeth to protect his mouth from injury. Such horses are often called *hardmouthed*.

A Foal that Bites

It's entirely normal for a foal to nip at you, but does that mean that you should accept this behavior? Not a chance!

When a foal gets a little rough while nursing, its mother will often swing her head around and give the foal a little nip in that area of loose skin behind the front leg, where the girth strap will someday go. Trainer GaWaNi Pony Boy recommends using a similar technique if a foal should nip you.

> When we're working with horses under six months old, and we get nipped—because it's natural—grab a patch of that skin with a full fist and give it a little twist. And immediately the ears perk up and they say, "Oh, that feels just like when Mom used to bite me when I was nursing a little rough." We always have to fall back on what horses would do; then, we try to re-create it.

As with most trainers practicing natural horsemanship, Pony believes that learning and practicing the language that horses use among themselves is the best way to motivate them.

Trainer's Confidence

Before you can successfully deal with horse-training issues, you need to have self-confidence. But where does that come from?

Success breeds confidence, but you need confidence to be successful. It's a timeless and frustrating paradox for anyone hoping to excel at just about anything. A horse trainer's confidence is especially important because it tells the horse that the trainer is competent to be the leader. But being confident doesn't mean you always have a ready answer, as dressage authority Mike Schaffer explains.

> Eventually you get to the point where you realize, You know what? No matter how bad this problem is, I'll be able to figure it out. And I don't need to get upset. Okay, maybe I can't fix it today, but I'll be able to fix this problem if I just sort of stay loose and think about it.

Horses don't know that *you* don't know unless you *act* like you don't know. On the road to being a horseman, you learn to "fake it until you make it."

🐴 Safety Position

Horses can react in ways that seem random and unpredictable to us humans. So how do we protect ourselves?

Every horse is an individual with a unique history of experiences that causes him to behave as he does. Sometimes that behavior can be life-threatening for the human that must handle him. Equine veterinarians face this every time they examine a strange horse, and most have developed their own methods for minimizing the chance of being kicked or bitten. For Dr. Robert M. Miller, every procedure starts from what he calls the safety position:

> The safest place to stand is always at the shoulder. As long as you're at the shoulder, the only injury you can suffer is getting your feet stepped on, which is never fatal.

When facing forward at the shoulder, you can see the horse's facial expressions and judge his attitude. When facing backwards, you can use your peripheral vision to pick up his head movement, and your elbow to block if his head comes around.

Training Deadlines

A sage bit of training advice is to "let it take the time it takes," but that doesn't mean you can't have deadlines.

It's good to let things unfold at their own natural pace, but you need a goal if you're going to progress with your horse. A deadline is simply a goal with a time frame attached, and that isn't always bad, says clinician Clinton Anderson.

> It's real easy for people that do what I do for a living to say that deadlines are bad and that they put too much pressure on your horse and all that kind of stuff. And to some degree, that is true. But you know what? If you do want to compete, there's got to be a day when you finish training and go and show what you have worked so hard to do. The key is to pick a deadline that's not unrealistic, and don't say, "I'm going to train him in a month." Say instead, "I'm going to train him in two years."

Sadly, that isn't always possible. The performance world is enamored with young horses, and trainers have no choice but to accelerate their training to be ready for key events.

Changing Approach

You need the patience of a saint to train horses, but even a saint has to know when to give up and try something different.

When we're teaching horses something new, they often don't give us the response we want immediately. Persistence usually wins out, but not always. Good trainers are on the lookout for signs that a different approach is needed. American Horse Trainers Group founder, Clay Harper, explains:

> If you're pushing a horse over the top, if the emotions are coming up too high—let's say you're doing round pen work and that horse wants to climb out of that round pen—that may not be the right tool for that horse, or you're putting too much pressure on that horse. You know, there are very sensitive horses, there are pushy horses, there are dull horses, and the same technique might not work for all three.

Having several different methods under your belt is just plain smart. Most bad experiences come when the owner simply runs out of ideas and too often, patience as well.

Backing Off the Cue

Ever wonder how great riders guide their horses with no apparent effort? You can do it, too. Just follow the steps.

For horsemanship clinician John Lyons, horse training is all about teaching horses to respond to cues. But it goes beyond that. John wants communication to become so refined that it's nearly undetectable to the observer.

> Whatever cue I'm giving, wherever I'm giving it, I want to continually back off of the cue and try to give it less and less. I don't expect less movement or action from the horse; I expect the same amount of movement, but I shouldn't have to work so hard to get it.

For example, the cue to turn left might start out as a pull on the left rein coupled with a press of the right leg against the barrel. Eventually, John would accomplish the same thing by just shifting his weight slightly in the saddle and thinking about going to the left.

Constant Maintenance

Training horses is like fixing cars. A good maintenance program goes a long way toward avoiding breakdowns.

Most horses will look and act pretty sharp after some intensive training, but it quickly wears off if the owner doesn't practice routine maintenance. These are the little things you do that remind your horse who's in charge. Native American trainer and educator GaWaNi Pony Boy offers this example:

> Every time I walk near my horses, I require them to turn around and face me. If they don't face me, I chase them away from me. And this is if I'm feeding, if I'm doing whatever around my barn. I might walk past my horse and touch him on the shoulder and ask him to lift his foot for me. I might be walking past my horse and touch him on the poll and expect him to drop his head. It's constant reinforcement and maintenance.

Don't think of your horse as ever being "off duty" and free to disobey you. That wouldn't be tolerated by the alpha horse in a herd, and it shouldn't be tolerated by you.

Squeeze, Cluck, Spank

Common wisdom is that when you want a horse to go faster, you kick him in the side. But does that really work?

If I poke you in the side, your body will contract instantly. The same thing happens when you kick a horse: His body contracts and his stride elevates and shortens. But to go faster, his stride must lengthen. Trainer Clinton Anderson explains how he makes that happen.

> I don't kick to make him go faster; I gently squeeze with my legs. If my horse does not respond by moving forward, then I'm going to cluck. If he still doesn't respond, then I'm going to get the end of my mecate (or you can use a little dressage whip or whatever you want), and I'll just start to flap it from side to side and tap him on the hindquarters with it. I'll always start gently and then increase the pressure. That spanking motion makes a horse feel uncomfortable, so that he *wants* to go.

With consistent use of the squeeze, cluck, spank sequence, your horse will learn to speed up with just a little bit of leg pressure from you.

Getting Tough

The last thing you want to do is constantly nag your horse. Getting tough is actually a kinder thing to do.

We've all seen parents who threaten their children when they misbehave, but never make good on those threats. These children become unmanageable because they've been taught there are no consequences to wrong behavior. The same thing is true with horses. Australian clinician Clinton Anderson says you have to be willing to get tough . . . at least once.

> Once they know that you will follow through with a harder reprimand, you hardly ever have to do it. That's the interesting part about it—because they know that you will.

Getting tough doesn't mean getting cruel. Slapping a horse sharply on the rump with a rope or a fiberglass training stick can get the point across, if you display enough aggressive body language along with it. The horse must believe that you are willing and able to really hurt him. For you, this is merely an acting job.

Skeptical Horse

Chances are, your horse isn't stupid. He isn't mean. He's not even unpredictable. He's just skeptical.

It's a natural assumption for those new to horses—and an ever-present temptation for those who aren't—to assume that horses see the world as we do. From their position in the food chain to the physiology of their brains, horses are about as different from humans as could be. They're preoccupied from birth to death with simply staying alive. The late, great natural horseman Ronnie Willis explains:

> The horse is a natural-born skeptic. He's a coward at heart. He's claustrophobic, and boy, when things get too close, too tight, he becomes a full-throttle-aholic. Instantly! He doesn't think. He reacts.

Ronnie Willis will be remembered not only for the horses he trained, but the people he influenced, including renowned horseman Pat Parelli.

Control Myths

A halter and lead rope are useful tools in controlling a horse, but beware of two common myths surrounding them.

Myth #1 claims that a halter and lead rope are *necessary* for controlling a horse. Just watch any good round pen trainer and you'll see how he can control a horse's movement with body language alone. Myth #2 claims that a halter and lead rope are *sufficient* for controlling the horse. Clinician Dan Sumerel reveals the weakness in this assumption.

> If that horse were to blow up, if that horse freaks out, if he spooks, or if he just decides to flat-out leave, you're going to find out how little you are and how strong he is, and you may not have enough rope or enough *you* to hang onto the rope and stop him.

A human can control a horse only if the horse *chooses* to be controlled. The horse won't make that choice until he is convinced that, between the two of them, the human is more qualified to be leader—with or without a halter and lead rope.

When Things Go South

It's always best to end a training session on a good note, but sometimes you have to back up a bit to do that.

Part of the appeal and challenge of horse training is that horses are not machines. They don't always respond as we expect them to. When that happens, the trainer's experience tells him whether it's time to turn up the pressure or wait a bit longer. California trainer Richard Winters explains what he does when all else fails.

> If I'm really stuck and things are going south—they're not getting better, they're getting worse—maybe what I need to do is back up to a spot where I know I can get a positive change. Where was I just before things started to go south? When were things good? I want to change that horse's mind and attitude and freshen him up back at a good spot. And then quit.

This doesn't mean the training session was a bust. Any time spent reinforcing foundation training with a horse will make it easier to teach him more advanced maneuvers.

Yes Answer Cue

Horses don't wag their tails when you praise them, but they do learn better with consistent positive feedback.

Learning a new cue is a trial-and-error process for a horse. The trainer exerts pressure in a way the horse doesn't recognize, and the horse tries different responses until the pressure goes away. Trainer John Lyons feels that a *yes answer cue* speeds up the process.

> The cue can be anything, but it's a consistent way of saying to the horse, "That's it. Good job. That's the right answer." It's better than having just a void. The release of pressure is what the horse wants. That tells the horse he's on the right track, or that's what you want him to do. The yes answer cue confirms it.

Consistency is important. Whether you use a stroke on the neck, a scratch on the forehead, or something verbal as your yes answer cue, you need to do it exactly the same way every time.

How Much to Push a Horse

Pressure, whether physical or psychological, is an essential tool in horse training, but how much is too much?

Pressure and release are the yin and yang of horse training. Neither can do the job alone. The timing of the release may be the primary factor in how quickly a horse learns, but using the wrong type or amount of pressure can undermine the best of timing. It's a challenge faced by professional and amateur horsemen alike, as clinician Clinton Anderson explains:

> A lot of trainers push their horses too hard, and a lot of trail riders—nonprofessionals, people who don't make their livings from horses—back off a little too early. So you've got to get that happy medium there. You've got to push them till you feel like they're listening to you, but not so much that they feel like there's no escape.

A good rule of thumb is this: Use the least amount of pressure necessary to get the desired response, and offer release at the earliest sign of a try—preferably when the horse first thinks of trying.

Relaxed Horse

No matter what the riding discipline, a horse that is relaxed and mentally calm will perform better.

It's one of the most persistent myths in the horse industry: An excited horse will perform better in athletic competition. Top horsemen, like trainer, riding instructor, judge, and author Richard Shrake, know better.

> The relaxed horse trains the easiest. Not only can we frame him, we can supplely put together his gaits, straighten him out, get him to perform at 100 percent potential. The second he gets stiff, the second he gets heavy, we lose all that. It's like a car with no power steering or one flat tire. So the ultimate goal of any horseman has got to be a horse that is supple and soft and relaxed.

Even racehorses perform better when they save the adrenaline for the race. Those that use it up in the gate are rarely big winners.

Clinic Preparation

Want to get the most out of a riding or horsemanship clinic?
Consider this radical idea: Prepare before you go!

Horses are homebodies, and clinic time is often wasted
when they aren't mentally ready to work in a new and strange
place. If their eating and drinking patterns have changed, it's
even worse. Clinician Peggy Cummings has this suggestion:

> Ride the horse before you go to the clinic so that the
> horse is somewhat fit to be able to flex with the change,
> being away from home. Some people aren't used to taking
> their horses other places; sometimes it takes two, three
> days for the horse to settle, and that can take away a lot
> from focus and learning time.

At the very least, try to get your horse out of his regular
home routine. Take him for a walk away from the barn or a
ride in the trailer. Do things that will get him back in the
habit of focusing his attention on you.

Making Cues Specific

The success you have in training your horse depends to a large extent on how self-disciplined you are at the job.

John Lyons has built his very successful horse-training system around the use of cues. He likes the precision that it brings to communication between human and horse, and he urges his students to be very methodical in the way they approach teaching cues.

> A general goal leaves you lots of room and different ways to reach it. The more specific you are with your goal and what you're teaching, the clearer you will be to your horse, and that's important. So be very, very specific with your cues. Write it down. For example, when I start tapping the horse with the dressage whip, it means give me forward motion, a forward thought.

John emphasizes that a cue is something that has been taught to a horse, and is not just his natural reaction to a stimulus.

Six Doors

Horses figure out what we want them to do using trial and error, and it should never take more than five errors.

A horse can only go one of six directions at any given time: up, down, forward, backward, left, or right. The trainer's job is to make it clear which direction he wants. Clinician Richard Winters describes the mental process the horse goes through to figure this out.

> He sees within his mind's eye this panorama of doors, and he starts trying door handles, trying to find a way out. We wiggle that rope and he tries the up door by raising his head up, or maybe even rearing up. Or he tries the front door. It's our job to have five of those doors completely sealed off, and then one door swinging wide open with spotlights shining down on it. And when they step through there, whew—then everything gets comfortable.

In other words, we keep pressure on the horse through all of the wrong choices. When the pressure goes away, he knows that's what we wanted.

Vowels and Pressure

Starting gently and escalating pressure slowly is at the heart of natural horsemanship. To remember how, just think of vowels.

Horse trainer Bob Jeffreys uses the vowels of the English language—A, E, I, O, and U—as a mnemonic device for remembering to increase pressure gradually on a horse. For instance, if you want a horse to move over, you might *ask* by pressing lightly on his shoulder with your hand using a half pound of pressure, then you'd *encourage* with four pounds of pressure. Still no response? *Insist* with ten pounds of pressure.

> If he still didn't move over, you might use both hands, use fifty pounds of pressure and *order* him to move over. But the instant he would move, using any one of those four letters, you go to the *undo*, and the undo—the release of the pressure—tells him he got it right.

Why not jump immediately to the *order*? Because that's not how horses communicate with each other.

Directing a Horse's Movement

Like an actor on the set of a movie, your horse can be taught to accept your direction of his movement.

In a herd, a dominant horse establishes his or her position by getting other horses to move—forward, backward, left, or right. Movement is a horse's primary defense mechanism, so yielding control of it to another is an act of submission. We can use this fact to gain a horse's respect and get him in a learning frame of mind, as described by trainer Clinton Anderson.

> Every time you direct your horse in one of those four directions, and when he does that you reward him for it, you're basically showing him that not only can you make him move, but when he does move in the direction you want him to go, he'll get rewarded for it. So, in turn, that gets him waiting for the next command, and it gets him thinking in his mind in a positive way rather than a negative way.

Trainers use groundwork exercises to get a horse moving in all four directions.

Graduated Pen Sizes

Often horse training starts in a round pen, but opinions vary on the ideal size. Maybe everyone's right.

Texas clinician Van Hargis is known for his gift of gab and infectious enthusiasm about teaching horsemanship. Like many modern horsemen, Van starts a horse's training in the round pen. Uh, make that round *pens*.

> In my case, I'm spoiled to death at the house. We've got a 40-foot round pen we do a lot of our groundwork in. Then we graduate to a 60-foot round pen where it's a little bit more inviting for the horse to move. And then from there, we go to a 150-foot round pen. The roundness allows the horse continuity of movement. There are no corners, nothing there to stop him. We want the horse to move out freely. From the 150-foot round pen, I will graduate to a very large roping arena. From there we go to the big world, the big pasture. But again, we're just kind of graduating up in steps.

It's a habit inspired by a saying from Van's grandmother: "Inch by inch, life's a cinch. Yard by yard, life is hard."

Generalized Learning

Horses can be taught to do some pretty amazing things, but their learning process is different from ours.

Animal behaviorists have discovered that many animals, including horses, find it difficult to see the common denominators in different life situations. Horse trainer David Lichman has collaborated with Dr. Jennifer Hurley in her work with sea lions. He describes the procedure she uses with these marine mammals.

> I go to this spot and I train this behavior, and I train it until I feel like it is working pretty well. And then the next thing I do is move it over there, and chances are, it's not going to work. Now I do it over here and over there, but there'll be people watching. Now I do what's called a hand-off, and I say, "Can another trainer do the same behavior here, back at the original spot, now another context shift over here?"

The same principle works with horses. By repeating the training in different locations and under different conditions, the horse develops *generalized learning*.

Proactive vs. Reactive Partners

Want to have a better relationship with your horse? Think of it as a partnership, with one of you clearly in charge.

There is one clear-cut reason you must be the boss with your horse: your own safety. Too often, new horse owners think they can handle horses like big dogs. But treating a horse like a dog can get you in a lot of trouble. Natural horseman Bob Jeffreys has a better idea.

> We can't treat them like pets. We don't want them jumping up and putting their hooves on our shoulders, nipping for treats, and things like that. We want to treat them as a partner, but we want to be the *proactive* partner—that is, the one that's making the requests, and having the horse respond to that as the *reactive* partner.

The partnership aspect is important, because you will be working together to get the job done, whatever it may be. But the horse also needs to know which of you is the leader. It's how he's been wired by nature. If you don't step up and take that job, the horse will.

Defining the Cue

Do you really know what you're asking your horse to do when you give him a cue? Many riders don't!

There's an old expression: "If you don't know where you're going, you won't know when you get there." Defining your goals is important throughout life. If you don't have a clear idea of the result you want when you cue your horse, you'll confuse him and frustrate yourself. Popular clinician John Lyons offers this example.

> A lot of people say that if they kick their horse, it means go forward. But if the horse is already walking forward when they kick him, you'd have to say, "Well, why did you kick the horse? The horse is already going forward." So, the definition of our cue is really critical because it helps us define where the problem is.

In this example, John suggests that the cue should be, "Give me a definite, noticeable change in leg speed." Kicking, bumping, or squeezing with your legs would then be appropriate, whether the horse was moving or not.

First Saddling

Saddling a horse for the first time doesn't need to provoke a fight. Preparation and the right attitude can make it easy.

Horses have a tendency to be frightened when they experience new sensations. The first saddling is a good example. A horse needs to be prepared for the feeling of the girth strap constricting his belly. This can be done by rhythmically tightening and loosening a rope around his middle until he relaxes. Something being placed on his back can also be scary. Applying and removing a saddle pad, again with rhythm, deals with that fear. Doing all of this in a straightforward, honest way makes the first saddling as simple as any other. Trainer Van Hargis describes his approach:

> I don't baby the horse. When it comes time to saddle him, I get him ready with a rope; I get him ready with a saddle pad. When I get ready for the saddle, I'm going to saddle him as if he's been saddled a hundred times before.

The horse looks to us for reassurance. If we expect the first saddling to go smoothly, it usually will.

Tiring a Horse Out

As big and strong as a horse is, we can still ask too much of him, especially when he's young and still learning the basics.

Light horse breeds are started in training for riding between two and four years old, when their skeletal development is nearly complete. But they aren't fully grown, and, as trainer Richard Winters explains, you still have to be careful about overdoing it.

> That's an administrative decision that you—as a hopefully experienced colt starter—will have to make. Five minutes of the wrong thing is too long. Two hours of the right thing might be all right. So sometimes it's not the duration of time, but it's what we're doing in that time. The more intense, the more physical it is, the faster they'll begin to run out of air, and the faster their limbs will get tired. We need to be aware of that. But I think the most important thing is to look for tries. Look for positive things and try to quit on those positive notes.

Horses of any age also need time during their training sessions to mentally process what is going on.

 **Acceptable Try**

We're told when training horses to find and reward the slightest try, but sometimes the slightest try isn't enough.

When you ask something of a horse, you want an honest try from him, one that is the best he has to offer at that moment. If this is something new to him, you will accept a fairly clumsy attempt as long as it is in the general direction you want to go. But next time, you expect more. The teacher's definition of an acceptable try changes as the student learns. Clinician Clinton Anderson offers this example:

> A kid that's learning how to spell in grade one, if he spells some things wrong, you're not going to make a big deal about it, are you? You're going to accept that he's tried to get his name correct and so forth. If that kid's in grade three now and he can't spell his name correctly, you're going to take that quite a bit more seriously because you expect more of him.

You should expect more from your horse every day, too. You're not really asking him to try harder; you're asking him to build, with the same effort, on what he already knows.

Before a Horse Blows Up

Horses do some unpredictable things at times. But with experience, you'll feel it coming and know what to do.

It's important to understand the nature of the horse. He is programmed to take flight any time he becomes worried about his safety. A good rider reads the signs that trouble is brewing and takes preemptive action, as Virginia clinician Kenny Harlow explains.

> If I'm on a horse and I know he's about to blow, right away I'm going to get him thinking of me without the horse getting more upset; I'm going to get him relaxed. As quick as I can, I'm going to start changing directions. I'm going to turn to the right, turn to the left. I'm going to get him so busy thinking about what my next request will be, he'll forget what he was worried about to begin with.

Why does this work? Because horses can't process two thoughts at the same time. In other words, they can't multitask—at least, not the way we can. It's important that you practice these maneuvers with your horse ahead of time so that your requests are familiar and clear to him when he's upset.

Moderating Training

Is your horse getting tired of your training schedule? Take some advice from an old Greek philosopher named Aristotle.

Aristotle believed that the key to happiness and virtue is moderation in all things. In other words, avoiding extremes. So training a horse too much could be as bad as training him too little. Clinician Dan Sumerel has helped world-class competitors break out of training slumps by getting them to scale back or moderate their intense training schedules.

> Train the horse Monday, Wednesday, and Friday. Tuesday and Thursday, take him outside on a loose lead. Maybe sit on his back, bareback, and let the horse graze. Take him for a walk. What you are doing is interrupting this pattern of behavior to get this horse to *not* associate you with stress. Sometimes when you're around, things are active and sometimes when you're around, things are really lazy and easy and cool.

Aristotle would no doubt approve.

Unloading Problem

Getting a horse to load in a trailer can be a challenge, and sometimes, once he's in, he doesn't want to come out.

Trailer-loading strategies revolve around making it more comfortable for the horse to be inside the trailer than out. Some horses learn the lesson a little too well and decide they'll just stay in the trailer, thank you very much. Pulling on the lead rope doesn't usually help. Trainer Josh Lyons has an ingenious alternative.

> If the rope's coming back on the left side, toward the middle of the trailer, you tie it back to the back post and offset his nose no more than two to three inches, just enough to be uncomfortable, and leave. Come back in ten minutes, and the horse will be standing quietly outside the trailer.

Some horses take longer, but left alone, they will eventually come out. Incidentally, no matter how comfortable a horse feels in a trailer, he may never feel completely safe there. Claustrophobia is just part of his nature.

Headshy Horse

Headshyness is a common problem, and when they try to fix it, many horse owners just make matters worse.

The horse that throws his head up when you try to touch it is headshy, and that can make handling him a real battle. Fear may be the root cause, but after a while, headshyness simply becomes a habit. Aussie trainer Clinton Anderson works with the headshy horse in a halter and lead rope, and desensitizes him to activity around his head.

> I'll get to the side of him and stand at a 45-degree angle. That way I'm not directly in front of my horse, so that if he struck at me, he wouldn't get me. I might get my arm and just wave it back and forth, like, 10 or 15 inches away from his head. What I don't want to do is sneak around my horse and just gently bring my hand up and rub him on his face; the more you sneak around them, the worse they get.

In desensitizing, it's important to continue the stimulus until the horse relaxes. Stopping too soon rewards the wrong behavior.

Getting a Horse's Attention

In order to get a horse to do what you want him to do, you must first get his attention, right? Not necessarily.

John Lyons is known as America's Most Trusted Horseman, a title earned by more than twenty years of helping people with their horses. He feels that getting your horse focused on you is not the first step in a training procedure.

> Not in any situation does the horse's attention come before his performance. Think about working a horse in a round pen. First few minutes, you get him to go around in the round pen. Do you have his attention? Or is he hollering or thinking about the other horses; or is he thinking about getting the heck out of that round pen? You don't have his attention, but you are getting him to do what you want. Get him physically to do what you want, and then what will happen is eventually, you'll have his attention.

According to John, the trainer's attention must come first, then the trainer's performance, followed by the horse's performance, and finally, the horse's attention.

Trainer's Syndrome

Just how far should you push a horse? How much should you ask of him during a training session?

To teach a horse anything, you apply pressure, either physical or psychological, to cause movement. When he makes an effort in the right direction, you reward the try by removing the pressure. The release is what teaches, and sometimes that release needs to include time for the horse to just stand, rest, and mentally process what happened. Unfortunately, this step is often skipped. Parelli Natural Horsemanship premier instructor and gaited horse specialist, David Lichman, explains:

> We call it the trainer's syndrome. "That was a great three steps of gait there; let's go for four!" And then you might get four and then you say, "Let's go for five!" If your program is always to go until it fails and then stop, then your program needs to change. You need to start thinking about, "I've got a habit here that's a bad training habit. I'm always destroying what I build."

Women and Horses

By most estimates, the horse industry in America is at least 70 percent female. What is it with women and horses?

Okay, they have the better body type for riding. With a wider pelvis and a lower center of gravity, the average woman is shaped better for riding than the average top-heavy man. That nurturing instinct generally works to their advantage, too. But women also have tendencies that don't help a bit on the road to becoming a horseman . . . make that horseperson. Trainer Clinton Anderson provides this insight:

> They have pretty decent rhythm and they start really gently, but that's where they stay. And the horse is like, "Well, it's going to take more than that to convince me that I need to move for you now." So they need to learn that it's okay to get more aggressive with your horse. Just because you get more aggressive with a horse doesn't mean that you don't love it anymore. You can still love an animal and take good care of it, and still be ready to support it and discipline it if necessary.

Losing Your Temper with a Horse

Horses can be frustrating, and it's easy to lose your temper with them . . . until you have some knowledge under your belt.

For John Lyons, every horse-training task has a certain number of steps to it. Follow the steps and when you get to the end, you'll get the result you want. Problem is, most folks don't know the steps, or feel that they should be able to skip a few to speed up the process. Then they lose their tempers when they don't get the results they want. John offers this analogy:

> Can you imagine driving out of Phoenix, trying to get to Houston, and getting to Tucson and losing your temper because you're not in Houston? Wouldn't make any sense at all, would it, when you know you have to go through all these towns before you're going to get to Houston? The person throws a fit in Tucson when they're lost on the freeway, and they have no idea where to go, what road to take—and they're still not in Houston.

When you know what to expect along the way, whether in the training pen or on the highway, you're not as likely to lose your temper.

Laying a Horse Down

It's a trick that will amaze your friends, but laying your horse down has practical benefits, too.

For trainer Ken McNabb, it started as a favor for a friend who couldn't climb up on his horse due to an injury. Ken taught the horse to lie down with his feet tucked underneath him, accept the rider, and then stand on cue. As he trained other horses to lie down, Ken noticed that this "trick" had another practical benefit.

> It does adjust the horse's mind a little bit, and it gets him trusting you a little more and thinking about you. He's a "fright and flight" animal, and when he lies down, he has to trust you. Even in a herd environment, everybody doesn't sleep all at once. Somebody's always on their feet to sound the alert, and that's kind of what happens. He lies down and he has to trust you to sound the alert if something's going to go wrong.

Lying down could be the ultimate expression of the horse's acceptance of your leadership, because in his mind, he's putting his life in your hands—and he's doing it on cue.

 **Foundation**

No matter how fancy the house, if it doesn't have a good foundation, you'll have problems. It's the same with a horse.

Horse trainers often harp on the need for a good foundation on a horse, and when there are problems with more advanced work, they nearly always go back to foundation exercises to solve them. But what is this foundation, and how does it vary from horse to horse? Arizona trainer and *Starting Colts* author Mike Kevil explains:

> Every horse I ride, I give him the same foundation. They
> need certain things. All horses need to learn to move away
> from pressure; that's the one thing we teach them. We just
> teach it to them in hundreds of different ways. And then we
> start combining those ways to get different maneuvers.

Pressure can be exerted physically or mentally. Either way, foundation training teaches a horse what he must do to get the pressure to stop. It's a simple but essential concept.

Horse Lowering his Head

More than any other physical indicator, the position of the horse's head tells you how calm he is.

When a horse is afraid, the first thing he does is raise his head, where he has the best view of his surroundings and can take flight if necessary. Conversely, when a horse lowers his head to the ground, usually to eat or drink, he feels safe enough to put himself in this vulnerable position. Popular clinician John Lyons explains how to calm your horse by getting him to lower his head.

> You can teach any horse to put his nose on the ground with a halter in about fifteen minutes by just putting two pounds of pressure on the halter rope. Then, when the horse takes his head up, keep the two pounds of pressure on. The instant that you see or feel or think the horse is thinking about dropping his head, you release the lead rope. And then you start repeating that, and within five minutes, the horse starts to understand that every time you start to touch the lead rope, he should drop his head a little bit.

Try it. It works!

Being at the Front

One of the most common problems reported by trail riders is the horse that always wants to be at the front of the group.

Many of the irritating habits our domestic horses have are rooted in natural herd behavior. If something scares a herd of wild horses, they'll take off en masse to escape the perceived danger. As trainer Clinton Anderson explains, no horse wants to be at the back of the herd at times like that.

> They're all trying to get to the middle or the front of the pack. Whoever's at the back and whoever's at the sides has the biggest chance of getting eaten. So, you know everybody's pushing their cousins and uncles and brothers to the outside, because they want them to get eaten first.

If your horse wants to go to the front during a trail ride, let him, but then pull off to the side and make him work, circling or doing serpentines, preferably at a trot. When the group has passed you, let him relax and rejoin the group. Soon he'll realize the back's not such a bad place to be.

CHAPTER THREE

Riding

One-Rein Stop

Being stuck on a runaway horse is the biggest fear of most riders. The one-rein stop can change all that.

To do the one-rein stop, the rider pulls on one rein instead of two. This bends the horse's head and neck to one side, making it hard for him to keep running forward. For the rider, this is not a difficult maneuver, as the horse has relatively little strength in his neck to oppose lateral movement. But the true magic occurs when the horse is *conditioned* to this cue ahead of time, as Dr. Robert M. Miller describes.

> A conditioned response is an involuntary response. It's working on the subconscious mind, which overrules the conscious mind. So even though he wants to run straight away, if you have established as a conditioned response that, when this horse feels this pressure, he's going to bend his head laterally all the way around, basically, it pulls him to a stop.

As he's slowing down, the horse will veer off to one side, so be sure you allow space for that.

Emergency Dismount

You've learned the proper way to mount and dismount a horse. Now here's what you really need to know.

When you're riding a horse, safety sometimes dictates getting off quickly. Clinician GaWaNi Pony Boy teaches the emergency dismount. Here, he explains when he would use it.

> If I see that the situation has gone out of control, I will bail out. If the saddle is coming off, I'll get off the horse. If I see a train in front of us, I'm out of there. And the other time you use it is when you're coming off and you don't mean to. When you're hanging off the side of the horse saying, "I'm going to fall now," it would be good if you could get out safely.

To do the emergency dismount, get your feet out of the stirrups, lean forward, kick your feet out behind you, and push off the horse's neck. Often you will land on your feet. If not, tuck and roll when you hit the ground. Usually, it's best to simply let go of the reins.

Scary Object on the Trail

It's lurking in the back of every trail rider's mind: What will I do if my horse balks at something on the trail?

It's embarrassing, frustrating, and sometimes dangerous when your horse decides a tree stump is a threat to his well-being. Trainer Clinton Anderson says not to pressure the horse, but to simply get his feet moving. Put him to work.

> The more I turn his feet left and right, forward, and backward, the more I get his respect. The more I get his respect, the more his emotions stop running away with him. So, by the time I get all that accomplished, he'll usually be huffing and puffing, and he's kind of worked for a few minutes, and then I let him rest beside the stump. Well, then the stump's not scary anymore because it was only scary when he had nothing to do with all that energy.

Two things are going on here. One, giving the horse something else to think about gets his one-track mind off what is scaring him. Second, by causing him to move, you're reinforcing your role as leader and showing he can trust you for his safety.

Inconsistency of Cues

No matter how willing and capable your horse is, you can sour his attitude quickly if you are inconsistent.

Imagine living someplace with no traffic laws, where a policeman could give you a ticket whenever it suited him. You wouldn't want to live there! Yet that's what you do to your horse when you are inconsistent in your expectations. National dressage champion Lendon Gray explains:

> What is so unfair is if today you ride around, kind of going bang, bang, bang on his side to get him going, or you use your leg and nothing really happens and you live with it and ask three more times. And then tomorrow you say, "Okay, today you're going to be on the ball!" That's what makes so many horses sullen and difficult: the inconsistency.

Lendon suggests giving cues with an escalating degree of firmness: a press of the leg, then a kick, then a smack with the riding crop. Applied consistently, horses soon learn to respond to the subtlest of cues.

Preparing the Feet

Sometimes our feet aren't exactly where they should be, and we stumble or lose our balance. It can happen to horses, too.

It's a sure sign of maturity as a horseman when you begin to look at things from your horse's point of view—and that includes the placement of his feet. The good rider times his cues so that it's easy for the horse to respond; his feet are in the right place to do what you're asking, as clinician Chris Cox describes:

> Ultimately, it's the feet that communicate with the ground. When you ask your horse to stop or to turn around, you've got to allow that horse enough preparation to get all those four feet just where he wants them, to be able to do that maneuver. So feel those four feet come up underneath your seat. Know where the diagonals are moving to, and feel that without looking down.

Looking down is a no-no; not because it's cheating, but because it moves your weight around on the horse's back, forcing him to rebalance himself. Kind of like you do when you are carrying a squirming toddler on your shoulders.

Riding Double

Many of us remember riding double on a horse as kids. Those of us who didn't get bucked off were just plain lucky.

The horse is better suited to pulling heavy loads than to carrying them. Still, we humans have been riding horses for nearly six millennia, and sometimes we make it harder than it needs to be. Like riding double. Anatomy expert Susan Harris points out how a second rider stresses the weakest part of a horse's back.

> That part of the horse's spine has no support. Farther back, it has support from the pelvis and the hind legs, and farther forward, it has at least some support from the ribs. But the horse's back gets weaker the farther back you go. Those back ribs, and especially his lower back or lumbar spine, or what we call the loins—that is not a good place for a horse to carry weight.

The heavier the horse's build, the more easily he can carry a second rider. But that should still only be done in emergencies.

Conditioning for Older Riders

Being fit is especially important if you're an older rider, and it can make a huge difference in your enjoyment of the sport.

A fitness regimen for older riders is no different in principle from that for older horses, as Dr. Jessica Jahiel, author of *Riding for the Rest of Us*, explains:

> Treat yourself the way you would treat your horse. Use intelligent conditioning methods. If you had a horse that you would just get out and gallop all over creation when he was six or seven, and now he's seventeen or eighteen and he's slowed down a bit, it doesn't mean you can't go out and have a great time. But you're going to need a longer warm-up, and you might want to spend more time walking and trotting and less time going "Yee-Haw" around the countryside.

There's no shame in slowing your daily run to a jog, or that jog to a brisk walk. Take a little more time warming up and stretching. And don't beat yourself up if you can't do everything you used to do. After all, you're only human.

Voice Training Before Riding

Teaching a horse to give to pressure must be done before you ride him. You might also teach him a few voice commands.

Growing up as an animal trainer in the circus, British horsewoman Tanya Larrigan has always believed in voice training, and has taught her young horses to respond to her voice, right along with learning to lead and moving away from pressure.

> Really, it's all word association for the movement you're doing. We actually start voice training in the stable, and then we want the horse to know his words before we actually mount him. He'd know his name, to halt, to wait, and to come here.

Voice commands are of obvious value when working a horse at liberty. When you're ready to ride him, voice commands can help set up the horse for gait transitions to come. And of course, having a repertoire of voice commands will help if you and your horse ever decide to run away and join the circus.

Ripple Effect

A good rider looks at ease on a horse's back because he is allowing the horse's energy to ripple through him.

Clinician Richard Shrake helps people eliminate resistance, both in their horse's behavior and in their riding technique. Resistance, or stiffness in a rider's body, interferes with what he calls "the ripple effect." He provides these examples.

> You've all watched riders that look like a woodpecker. Their upper body just pumps on a horse. They're generally really stiff in their hips, and that energy flow stops there. Riders that kind of bounce on their horse's back like a rock skipping on a pond? They're riders that generally are really stiff in their knees, and so, instead of softening their knees and their back, the stiffness there blocks that energy so they bounce.

Once they understand the concept of energy flow, many people can ride surprisingly well with just one lesson.

Collected Stride

True collection is a difficult thing to achieve with a horse, and many people don't really understand what it means.

Collecting, in the simplest terms, is when a horse shifts his weight back and brings his hind legs more under his body. Dressage champion Lendon Gray explains how collection affects the horse's stride.

> It isn't shortening the stride. The horse moving in collection moves very big, but it's a higher, rounder stride as opposed to a longer, lower stride. You have really the same amount of movement that you have in a horse that's moving free; it's just been put into a rounder, higher space.

Collection can't be turned on and off like a lightbulb. The muscles of the back and hind end must be conditioned over time to do the job, and in performance, a good dressage rider will ask the horse to collect a little at a time rather than all at once.

🐴 Leg Aids

Horses and riders come in all shapes and sizes. A rule of thumb for matching them up is where the rider's calf falls.

Traditional riding form is to sit straight in the saddle with head, shoulders, pelvis, and heels in vertical alignment. The legs are extended directly below the body, with the lower leg behind the girth. Elongation of the lower leg improves the rider's balance and the effectiveness of leg cues, as champion rider Lynn Palm explains.

> If you take his top line, which is up on his back, and his under line, which is under his belly, and cut him in half, the horse's sensitivity to communication through your leg aids is on the lower half of his barrel; so the longer your leg is, the easier it will be for you to connect with a sensitive part of his body, to better communicate with the horse.

Unfortunately, youngsters competing in the show ring are often mounted on horses too big for them to use their legs effectively.

Looking Ahead

Your hands, legs, posture—there are lots of things to think about when you start riding, but your eyes may be the most important.

Think back to when you first learned to ride a bicycle. You probably began with your eyes focused on the handlebars or the front tire, but after you got the hang of it, your gaze was well out in front of you, taking in the world and focusing on where you were going. The same thing happens when you learn to ride horses, says clinician Chris Cox.

> Looking ahead would be one of the biggest things that I would ever promote about general riding. Looking ahead, and not looking to try to see what lead you're on, or how good you look in the shadow that's beside your horse. Feel that feeling.

Don't forget that the head has weight to it, and when a new rider is looking all around, his center of gravity is constantly changing. The horse feels this. Experienced riders tend to be quieter in the saddle, and when they do move, they remain balanced while doing it.

The Training Scale

Rhythm, suppleness, contact, impulsion, straightness, and collection. Together they make up the Training Scale.

The Training Scale gives riders a plan of attack for developing a horse and dealing with problems that may arise. Let's say you're trotting around and everything's going great, but when you attempt a leg yield, it all falls apart. Your horse starts throwing his head, stiffens his back, and his rhythm becomes irregular. American dressage legend Jane Savoie says the Training Scale holds the answer.

> Most riders think, "Oh, the head's in the air. Gotta get the head down." They try to fix the contact first. No. You fix it in the order of the Training Scale. Get the regularity of the rhythm back first, the suppleness second, then you fix the contact. When ingredients are falling apart, you put them back in the order of the Training Scale.

Jane describes the Training Scale as a formula for training that applies regardless of the riding discipline.

Building Focus

The power to focus is one of the keys to success at anything, including riding. But how do you develop your focus?

One of the principles clinician Charles Wilhelm learned along the way is that you have to start where you are, not where you aren't. Building your focus while riding is a perfect example. Charles shares this method with his students.

If you know that you can have focus for five minutes, give your focus for five minutes, then stop your horse, think about what you've got to do at home—getting groceries or the kids or whatever—and then go back to your focus again. Then try to do it for six minutes, seven minutes, until finally you reach a goal; it's very doable that way.

Why worry about focus while handling a horse? Because you are asking the horse to trust you to be in charge of the team. If you are not thinking about the task at hand, the horse will know it and become confused or worried about his safety—and then, behavior problems are not far behind.

Horse for a Heavier Rider

A heavier rider needs to take special care in picking his or her mount, and a shorter horse may be best.

Dr. Jessica Jahiel is a beloved author, teacher, and cheerleader for countless beginning riders. She finds that heavier riders often pick the wrong kind of horse.

> A lot of riders look at themselves and say, "Oh my gosh, I'm too heavy, and I think I'd better go get something that's seventeen hands because then I'm going to look better and he'll be a taller horse, so he can carry me better." Wrong. Usually, the horse that you want is a good weight-carrying horse. A nice, sturdy, strong, good-boned horse, and a lot of those are going to be in the fifteen hands area.

Take a look at Icelandics, Haflingers, and all of the stock horse breeds. You'll find bigger-barreled, larger-boned individuals of moderate height that can easily carry your weight. They'll be easier for you to mount, and you'll look just fine.

Horse Camping Equipment

If you're a serious backpacker, you probably already have most of the gear you'll need to go horse camping.

The *Go light* and *Leave no trace* mantras of backpacking are also those of today's horse campers. Both sports use much of the same ultramodern equipment, as backcountry horseman Don West explains.

> The tents, the sleeping bags, the sleeping pads that we use, the stoves, pots, and pans; all of those pieces of equipment are right from the backpacking market. And they've already designed things that are so ultralight, very comfortable, and easy to use. They actually take a lot of the hassle out of backcountry travel.

Instead of using one large pack, the horse camper uses multiple small packs that fit neatly on the front and back of the saddle, allowing him to take trips lasting several days without bringing an additional pack animal, and without wearing a pack himself.

Five-Gaited Saddlebred

Walk, trot, and canter are the three gaits we associate with horses. But the American Saddlebred can learn two more.

The American Saddlebred originally resulted from crossing Narragansett Pacers and Thoroughbreds. Saddlebreds are born with the ability to walk, trot, and canter, and they can learn the slow gait and the rack, which are based on the pace. Saddlebred judge Gayle Lampe puts in perspective the five gaits of today's Saddlebred show horse.

> For Saddlebred horses, we collect them very much and have a very slow, rocking horse canter. So next to the walk, the canter would really be the slowest. The slow gait, done correctly, should be very, very slow. The trot and the rack should both be very fast, one not necessarily faster than the other.

Interestingly, the five-gaited Saddlebred is not classified as a gaited horse. That term is reserved for horses that have an intermediate gait *instead* of a trot.

Concessions to Age

It happens to every one of us without fail: We get older, and that means making some compromises.

Riding is one of the few athletic endeavors that you can safely and enjoyably pursue throughout your entire life. But as you get older, plan on making a few concessions to age. Eighty-one-year-old endurance rider Julie Suhr shares her experience:

> You have to accept a certain amount of humiliation that in your younger years you thought you would never put up with. If you have to have a milk crate to climb up on your horse, so what, as long as you get on top of him? That's where you want to be, and it doesn't matter what people think.

Saddling your horse can become a challenge, too, and getting a lighter saddle will only help for a while. Eventually you might want to try something creative, like California horseman Bill Dorrance did. At the age of ninety-three, he was still hoisting a big Western saddle onto his horse every day using a pulley system attached to a rafter in his barn.

Bucking Brakes

What do you do if a horse starts bucking with you on his back? Why, just use your bucking brakes, of course.

Horses buck out of fear, pain, habit, or orneriness. Unless you're a rodeo cowboy, you probably want nothing to do with a horse that bucks. Still, you may someday find yourself on one. Trainer Doug Babcock offers this advice for when that happens.

> It's best to know which side of your horse responds quickest to your rein, and we're talking about just using one rein at a time here. If he's already bucking and you're up there, the best thing to do is just grab a rein and give it a good heave until you feel his front feet stop and his hindquarters swing around.

Pulling on one rein brings the horse's head to one side, taking away much of his power and forcing him to step to the side to maintain his balance. Hold the head in that position until the horse relaxes and you can safely dismount.

Breathing to Slow and Go

Most people kick to go and pull back to stop, but there's a better way to tell your horse what you want him to do.

When you ride a horse, he's tuned into your physical state more than you probably realize. When you hold your breath, from fear or anxiety, he feels it, and some of that emotion is transferred to him. Regular, even breathing is one way to reassure your horse, and special breaths can actually work like cues. Riding instructor and natural horsemanship clinician Julie Goodnight explains:

> Inhaling is associated with movement, and it gathers the energy in your body. Exhaling is associated with stopping and slowing down and relaxing. So if you use your breathing when you're communicating to the horse, and inhale on an upward transition and exhale on a downward transition, just your breathing alone will cause a reaction in your body that the horse can feel.

Posting on the Diagonals

The trot is arguably the hardest gait to ride well, but we can take a lesson from great cavalries of the past.

Faster than a walk and less strenuous for the horse than a canter, the trot was the gait of choice for many cavalry maneuvers. To minimize pounding on the horse's back, it was recommended that the rider post, or stand slightly in the stirrups with each stride. Clinician Curt Pate describes how the technique was put into practice:

> When you're posting, it's easier for the horse to bring that foot up underneath himself. And if you were posting on the right diagonal all the time, then pretty soon the horse would be reaching farther with his right. So you would switch diagonals to keep your horse balanced. That's what they said in the cavalry. I think there is so much in the cavalry days—the U.S. Cavalry and the French Cavalry. Those folks were such good horsemen; a lot of things they did should be brought back up.

The trot is a two-beat gait. Each front leg moves in sync with the back leg on the other side. The two pairs of legs are called diagonals.

Waiting for Impulsion

Impulsion is one of the holy grails of horsemanship, but there are times when impulsion can be a bad thing.

It's generally defined to mean moving forward with power, so impulsion is obviously a very important thing to have when competing with your horse. Still, there are other things that need to be mastered first, according to famed dressage rider and coach Jane Savoie:

> When you ask for impulsion, you're asking for more of whatever qualities you already have, so you'd better like what you have. If your horse is irregular in the rhythm, if he's stiff rather than supple, if he's against your hand, not taking a good contact, and you ask for power, you ask for impulsion—you will get more irregularity, more stiffness, more against the hand.

It's like driving a car with a big engine. Before hitting the gas, you need to be sure the steering works, the tires have air, and the wheels are in alignment.

Kicking up at a Canter

Many horses today are overfed and underworked, so it's not unusual for them to resist cantering.

Trainer Clinton Anderson asks for the canter from a trot with a squeeze of the leg. If there's no response, he clucks. If there's still no response, he spanks the horse rhythmically behind the saddle. Some horses show their displeasure by kicking up.

> If that's all they're doing, it's no big deal. I'll just spank them again. Every time they kick up, I just spank them with the end of the rope—bang, bang, bang—and go on. So it's kind of like, "I get it. Every time I kick up, a bee stings me on the top of the tail." And I'll do that consistently until they quit it.

Clinton suggests holding onto the saddle horn or pommel with your free hand to help keep your seat. If you'd rather, you can spank the horse in front of the saddle. It's less effective, but reduces the chance he'll kick up. Incidentally, kicking up is not bucking, and it's more common with docile horses that have simply become lazy.

Balance Position

Riding is made easier by being balanced in the saddle, and that comes from keeping your body in alignment.

Ears, shoulders, hips, and heels. When these body parts are aligned, you are sitting in the balanced position in the saddle. Riding instructor Julie Goodnight talks about what happens to this alignment at various gaits.

> Walking or standing still, this alignment is vertical or perpendicular to the ground. When you're trotting and cantering, it may also be vertical, but sometimes we ride in a more forward position; for instance, when you're jumping or galloping really fast. But you would still have your shoulder, hip, and heel alignment. It's just that that line, instead of being perpendicular, would then be canted forward at the top and back at the bottom.

A barrel racer is a good example. She may be leaning forward as she races to the next barrel, but her legs are back, maintaining the alignment.

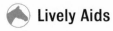 **Lively Aids**

Which would you rather have when you ride—a dull, lifeless horse, or a lively horse that you can control?

Every horse is a unique individual with his own energy level. Breed and age have something to do with it, but just about any horse can be taught to move with purpose and life. American dressage clinician Mari Monda Zdunic explains:

> If your horse is, let's say, a quieter, more phlegmatic horse, it would be up to you to encourage sparks in that horse, and that would take us back to those lively aids that the rider would have. It would take us back to not nagging your horse, not sitting heavy on your horse— having lively aids to produce a lively horse.

The same thing is true when you're handling a horse from the ground. There are times when you need to bring up your energy and have some assertiveness in your manner. Your horse will respond better to your commands and respect you more if you do.

Live Weight/Dead Weight

When it comes to riding, it's not how many pounds you're carrying; it's how you carry those pounds that matters.

According to Connected Riding creator Peggy Cummings, when you get connected in movement with your horse, you become live weight and are able to help your horse travel in balance, no matter how much you weigh.

> When you're not with the movement or when you're bracing or stiffening, your body is dead weight and it goes against the horse's movement. The horse has to work harder to carry you, and you have to work harder to make him do things, or you start learning mechanical ways to make him listen. Eventually, that takes a lot of toll on both the rider's body and the horse's body.

Relaxing your body and loosening your joints is key to getting connected with a horse, and it all starts in your mind.

Longe-Line Riding

Riding is much older in Europe than in the United States, and the way riders are usually started is different there.

Europeans have always taken their riding seriously, and doing it properly is very important to them. According to riding instructor Anna Jane White-Mullin, beginning riders are usually not given control of the horse. The instructor controls the horse via a long line, called a *longe line*, attached to the horse's headstall.

> They put people on a longe line and they longe them for a year before they allow them to even ride on their own at all, to develop their position so that their leg is correct, their seat is correct, their balance is correct. Then eventually they take up the reins and they ride—still on the longe line—and eventually, they let them off.

This may seem a safer way to start new riders, but it's no guarantee there won't be wrecks. And when things start falling apart, having an extra human and an extra line involved can actually complicate matters.

Thinking Back Toward the Rider

On trail rides, does your horse seem to be distracted? There's an easy way to get him thinking back toward you.

Think about how you drive your car. Even if the road is perfectly straight, your hands are continually making small adjustments in the steering. This is the secret to keeping your horse focused on you, rather than his surroundings, on a trail ride. Natural horseman Bob Jeffreys suggests the following strategy:

> If you want them to pay attention and think back toward you as the rider, ask them something every minute or so. And it doesn't have to be much. Just pick up the left rein, see if he'll give his jawbone to the left. So you look a little funny going down the trail—you're kind of going left and right—but at least your horse is paying attention, thinking back toward you and not thinking way out there: Where's the deer? Where's the hunter? Where's this? Where's that?

This technique relies on a very important fact: The horse's mind can only think about one thing at a time. If the horse is thinking about you, that's *all* he'll be thinking about.

Context of Cues

There are only a few cues that we can give horses, yet we expect them to do many different things. How do they figure it out?

Consider this example: To ask for a canter depart on the left lead, a rider will press with his right heel behind the girth. Yet this is exactly the same cue for moving the horse's hindquarters to the left. Trainer Bob Jeffreys explains how a horse sorts it all out.

> In one case, you start to ride the canter. You're looking out in the canter. You're thinking canter. Your shoulders are in the canter. Your arms are in the canter. It's a combination, and that's why it's so important that we do a lot of repetitions when we're teaching our horse, so they get used to that whole picture.

In other words, the context in which a cue is given makes all the difference in how a horse interprets it. Horses do seem to sense our intentions, but they aren't reading our minds; they're reading our bodies. So, be careful what your body is saying!

 **Adhesive Seat**

Not to get too personal, but how's your seat? You'll need a good one if you want to ride horses well.

Seats come in all sizes and shapes, but that doesn't really matter when you're riding a horse. What's important is how your tush sticks to the saddle. In riding, your seat and legs should meld with the horse; your torso, arms, and head should float, as if independent, above him. Dressage instructor Charles de Kunffy says a good seat will make all of the riding aids more effective.

> Once that rider has an adhesive seat that travels on the directional wave of the horse's oscillating back, the adhesive seat that doesn't sit on the horse, but *inside* the horse's movement—that rider has no difficulty with any of the aids.

With an independent, adhesive seat, riding looks nearly effortless. Without it, riding can look a lot like work.

Lips, Tongue, and Bars

The horse's mouth is a delicate, multitiered communication center, and the bit is your high-speed connection to it.

Veteran show horse trainer Richard Shrake teaches riders to have light hands, and to use subtle pressure on the bit when communicating with the horse.

> When that mouthpiece is in the horse's mouth, the first thing it's supported by is the lips, and they're very thin, like the icing on a cake. When horses are ridden lightly, they respond to their lips. They can have self-carriage. They can run their fastest. They can change leads their prettiest, because we're not getting to lean or brace on that bit.

Using heavier hands, or pulling harder on the reins, engages the horse's tongue and can cause him to travel with his weight too much on his front end, making it hard for him to perform well. Pulling harder still can cause painful pressure on the bars or gums, and the horse may bolt or rear.

Duration of Collection

It's something every serious rider tries to achieve with his or her horse, but collection is often misunderstood.

A horse that is collected is ready physically and mentally to perform at his best. His weight is shifted back with his hind legs under him, ready to push off. His front end is lightened so he can change directions if he needs to. And his mind is focused on what he is doing. Dressage clinician Mari Monda Zdunic feels that collection is a fleeting state that occurs when the horse's potential energy transforms into kinetic energy and performance.

> If we watch the horse turned loose, it would be the moment when the horse might have tucked under behind, his neck elevated, and he bolted or he did something. That's collection, which lasts a very short period of time. What we do is, we think our horse should remain collected for forty minutes, ten minutes, sixty minutes. That's not right.

Sawing on the Reins

Riding students sometimes resort to quick fixes to get the look they want their horses to have. It doesn't work.

There's a saying that "He who owns the hind legs owns the horse." Good riders know that the performance of the horse begins with his hindquarters, the motor, the source of his power. As dressage rider and instructor Jane Savoie puts it, you must ride the horse from the back forward. Inexperienced riders often focus on the front end of the horse.

> They do a very simple and very incorrect thing: sawing on the horse's mouth, where they alternate with their hands—left, right, left, right—and move the bit across the horse's mouth to bring his face in. That's a temporary, cosmetic, quick fix. And yes, your horse might have his neck down and his face in for the moment, but if you ride him from front to back like that, I guarantee you, when you go to do any kind of transition, that horse's head and neck are going to go up in the air.

The Rider's Outside Leg

You think of them as your left and right legs, but in riding, they're referred to as your inside and outside legs.

When your horse turns to the left or travels on an arc to the left, your left leg is your inside leg and your right leg is your outside leg. Going to the right, the leg functions are exactly reversed. Dressage master and author Charles de Kunffy describes the function of the outside leg:

> The outside leg bends the horse and makes sure that his quarters are closed. If the outside leg doesn't do its function, the horse will go through corners and bends like a sailboat goes around a light tower. The horse will swing his haunches out and skid out.

Different maneuvers require the outside leg to be in slightly different positions—sometimes in front of the girth and sometimes behind it. At times the leg exerts pressure, and at other times, it is simply a presence.

Continuum of Gaits

Most horses aren't asked to do more than three basic gaits: the walk, trot, and canter. But they can be taught to do more.

Every horse can perform a walk and a canter. It's what he does in between that gets interesting. It might be a bouncing trot or a swinging pace. These two-beat gaits are no fun to ride. Horses may also have four-beat gaits that lie on the continuum between the trot and pace, gaits such as the running walk, fox trot, rack, or tolt. These are much smoother gaits to ride, as Parelli Natural Horsemanship gaited horse specialist David Lichman explains:

> A person with an educated seat can maybe identify nine or ten different variations along that continuum, but as you know, there's an infinite number of points on a line, so the horse has, theoretically, an infinite number of gaits he can do if he has the propensity to do so.

In the hands of a skilled trainer, almost any horse can learn additional gaits, whether he has the genetic predisposition or not.

Ranch Roping

Arena roping has the speed and violence people love in football. Ranch roping is more like a game of chess.

On working ranches, cows are often roped while they're in the herd. The cowboy uses a long, supple rope and an arsenal of roping shots to get the job done with minimum commotion, as described by clinician Curt Pate.

> What we want to be able to do is throw from any position on the cow, from either side, from front, from back, so you can be out of that flight zone at any time and get your rope on him. If you have a real stiff rope, you've only got one shot, and that's from straight behind. A houlihan shot, which is a backwards shot that you can really throw a long ways—that's usually a one-swing thing. Some of the overhand shots you can swing a few more times, but the more you swing, the more chance you have of scaring the animal.

Cows are usually roped for branding or doctoring, so you want to keep them as calm as possible, and not burning up any extra calories. That is money down the drain for a cattle ranch.

The Safe, Short, and Smooth Horse

As we get older, most of us prefer comfort, reliability, and
safety in our automobiles—and in our horses.

Young riders tend to have better reflexes, balance, agility,
and strength than older riders. But that doesn't mean seniors
should give up on riding. It simply means a different sort of
horse is appropriate. Eighty-one-year-old endurance riding
legend Julie Suhr still pounds the trails, leaving riders half her
age in the dust—but she does it on 3S horses.

> I no longer want the ones that spook and dance and
> prance. I no longer want 15.1 or 15.2 horses; I want some-
> thing under 15 hands, because I find I can't get up on them
> otherwise. And I want the one whose trot is just naturally a
> very comfortable trot, a smooth trot. What I need is what's
> called the 3S horse—the safe, short, and smooth horse.

Julie's life story is contained in her book, *Ten Feet Tall, Still*.

European Rulers

Riding builds character, which is why the nobility of traditional Europe was raised on horseback.

Born in Hungary, living now in California, dressage master Charles de Kunffy speaks three languages and is known throughout the world for his writing and teaching. He offers this insight as to the role of the horse and riding among the elite of Europe:

> The horse gives the rider courage, and the horse gives the rider empathy, focus, self-discipline, and a sense of justice. So the ruling classes became appropriate rulers on horseback, not because of the monks and the nuns that schooled them in the monastery.

De Kunffy points out that riding is not for the body only, but also for the mind and the spirit. In short, riding helps us become better people.

Student Mistakes

On the road to becoming a horseman, there's a lot to learn, and you're going to make mistakes. Get over it and move on!

If you really care about developing skills in any field, you're going to feel bad about making mistakes. That's only natural, but you need to put it in perspective. Linda Parelli of Parelli Natural Horsemanship shares her thoughts.

> I don't think students make mistakes. Part of learning is, you try and you fail and you try and you fail, but it's not a mistake. The only time you do make a mistake is when you know better, and as a student, you don't know better, so you're just trying the best you can and moving forward. Just look at it as learning; you're learning the good, the bad, the indifferent, and sometimes learning doesn't look that great. But once you've learned it, then it does look great, and then you can start practicing and perfecting it.

Fortunately for us, horses are very adaptable and forgiving creatures. They often sense our intent, even when we aren't clearly expressing it.

Cue vs. Conversation

To be successful in riding dressage, you need a continuous flow of communication between you and your horse.

For more than fifty years, Californian Peter Lert has immersed himself in the sport of dressage as an instructor and as a judge. He's grown to dislike the notion of giving the horse a cue to elicit a particular response. To him, dressage requires something different.

> In dressage, we try to establish a continuous rapport, a continuous connection with the horse. In a cue situation, you say this and then you wait for the horse to do that. That's really a different sequence than continually influencing the horse with your aids to say, "Now we're going to do this. Now we're going to do that." It's a conversation that doesn't stop and shouldn't be interrupted.

The natural aids are the hands, legs, and seat. The rider's focus can also be considered a natural aid.

Stopping with Exhale

Do you worry that a horse will run away with you? Here's a tool for stopping him—and it's one you have with you all the time.

For Peggy Brown, a Centered Riding and Driving instructor, a panicking horse elicits an unusual response. She takes a breath, then exhales slowly and deliberately. In her own experience, it has worked repeatedly to defuse a dangerous situation.

> I'm not going to tell you it's going to work every time. Each time it happens to me, it's like a miracle. It's just kind of keeping presence of mind, keeping calm with my own body, not panicking, and transferring that calmness, that communication to the horse, saying, "Whoa, it's okay. We can go on."

This technique works even when driving. The horse can feel the relaxation coming through the lines. By contrast, holding your breath causes tension and tightness, which the horse can also feel through the lines.

Easing into Speed

There are few fantasies more enticing to a horse lover than stepping into the irons and riding a really fast racehorse.

Jockeys make it look easy, but riding a racehorse at speed is no stroll in the park. *Backyard Racehorse* author Janet Del Castillo feels that's one more advantage to training your own racehorse: You get used to speed together.

> There's a whole package of factors that go into easing into speed, and the nice thing when you're training your own horse is that you learn how to ease into speed as he's learning how to do it. It's really scary if you get on a horse you've never ridden and he clicks into high speed, and you've never done it before.

Most jockeys ask a horse for speed by kissing to him, rocking forward over his neck, and taking a tighter hold of the reins. They don't use spurs, as spurring a horse shortens his stride. If needed, a jockey will use his crop to spank the horse, which causes him to lengthen his stride.

Overcoming a Horse's Panic

Inside every calm horse is one waiting to explode. You need to be prepared in case that should ever happen to you.

Like many modern clinicians, Clinton Anderson advocates pulling on one rein instead of two reins to stop a horse from running off or bucking. It's a move that needs to be practiced repeatedly at all gaits until it becomes second nature for both rider and horse.

> Horses are creatures of habit, so if you've done this one-rein stop hundreds and hundreds of times, when he goes to take off and he's using the reacting side of his brain, when you bend his head around, his brain says, "I know what this is. This means safety. This means I need to listen and respect my owner, and it means I'm not going to get hurt." Every other time you've done it, you've never hurt him, so it overrides his natural instinct to panic.

By invoking a pattern of behavior the horse has already learned, you get him thinking again instead of blindly reacting.

Western to English

Ever consider switching from Western to English riding? You can do it, but it takes more than just switching saddles.

Generally speaking, Americans ride Western or English. Saddle, bridle, bit, type of horse used—even the rider's clothing and attitude differ between the two styles. You can move from one to the other, but it will require some adjustment for your horse, as retraining expert Sharon Smith explains:

> I find that the easiest thing to do with a horse is to not give him too much at once. For example, if you've got a Western horse and you want him to go English, he's probably going to have to learn two things. He's going to have to learn to respond to the direct rein, and he'll have to learn that the saddle is different—and not just in appearance and weight. The rider's center of balance is also going to be a little bit different.

Most English riding is done in a snaffle bit, the same kind used to start young Western horses, so the bit change should be the easiest part of the transition.

Left Turn Prep

Turning a horse to the left is simple—just pull on the left rein, correct? Well, actually, there's a better way to do it.

Good riders give their horses an idea of what they're going to ask for before they ask for it. These preparatory commands are invisible to the observer and nearly subconscious to the rider, but they make a big difference all the same. Resistance-free riding guru Richard Shrake takes us through an example.

> We're going to turn to the left. The first thing we're going to do before we pull on his mouth is actually look to the left. Our upper body, like a periscope on a submarine, turns in that direction; we use our leg on him, and then we give him the signal. So, the preparatory command is the look, the upper body turn, and then the leg.

In this example leg pressure is used only on the horse's right side; in effect, "opening the door" on the left. Pulling on the horse's mouth may not even be necessary.

CHAPTER FOUR

Competing

Heidi Nyland

Match Races

Whether it's money or just bragging rights that are at stake, the match race is a time-honored American tradition.

Films have immortalized teenagers racing their cars on lonely highways, but virtually the same contests have been taking place for centuries with horses. Top racehorse trainer Blane Schvaneveldt remembers his own youthful match races.

> The neighbors would get to bragging about their horses, and pretty quick they'd have a match race with their saddle horses, or whatever they had. So we'd go down on an old dirt road and run them. No starting gate, just lap and tap. Just two horses and a guy that stands down there and tells you when to go. Get them as even as you can. Try to get a start on the other guy.

History is filled with colorful stories of match races that changed the fortunes of the people involved. Everyone loved speed, and a stud horse that could outrun all comers often became a highly profitable business.

Hunters vs. Jumpers

Hunters and jumpers are so often lumped together that they may seem to be one type of horse—but they're not.

Hunter classes in horse shows are rooted in the type of riding done on English fox hunts. Much of it is flat work, with occasional, relatively low jumps. Clinician Anna Jane White-Mullin explains how that differs from jumper classes.

> The hunters are judged on their way of moving and the smoothness of jumping style, and a good, clean jumping style: high legs and a round back, and having even steps between the fences. The jumpers are judged on how fast you can go through the course, how high you can jump, how tightly you can turn. Everything is an athletic feat. So one is more like ballet or the arts, and the other's more like a sport and an athleticism.

In the past, Thoroughbreds dominated hunter classes, and Thoroughbred/draft horse crosses, or warmbloods, were favored for jumping. Today a variety of breeds are being used.

Four-in-Hand Navigators

If you want to give four-in-hand driving a try, better line up a couple of good-sized friends. You'll need them.

Four horses don't sound like much when you're talking about an engine, but it's a whole lot of power when it's attached to a carriage. In fact, with four-in-hand driving, it's good to have a couple of linebackers on board just to keep the carriage on the ground, as international driving sensation Chester Weber describes:

> The carriage is four feet wide or so, and it weighs about twelve hundred pounds, so this is a really heavy, very narrow carriage, and the horses have a great degree of power. Those people actually lean to the right and to the left in the turns to keep the carriage from tipping over.

These extra riders are called navigators, because in addition to throwing their weight around, they help the driver stay on course during cross-country competition, the second and most grueling day of three-day driving events.

Racing Records

Nothing is more thrilling than a horse race, but as a sport, horse racing is really not going anywhere.

Every year, fans eagerly await the Kentucky Derby, the Preakness, and the Belmont Stakes, Thoroughbred racing's triple crown. The hoopla may be growing, but compared to human sports, horse racing is not getting any better. Natural horseman Pat Parelli explains:

> Racehorses have not been running any faster for over a hundred years. Every year in track and field and swimming, people break world records because of sports psychology, and sports psychology comes from the confidence and the dignity and the curiosity of, "What do I have to do inside myself to get myself to run faster?" When we discover equine sports psychology, that's when the records are going to start being broken again.

Parelli Natural Horsemanship aims to get horses to "run faster and jump higher through heart and desire," the application of sports psychology.

Eventing: Cross-Country

In the Olympic equestrian sport of eventing, there are three days of competition, but day two is the killer.

In three-day eventing, day one is dressage, day three is show jumping, and sandwiched in between is the day that usually determines the winner: cross-country. Eventing goes back to the testing of cavalry horses, and day two contains the meat of it, as described by multi-time Olympian David O'Connor.

> It would be just like in the old days, with a cavalry horse taking a message from one battlefield to another. What's he going to encounter along the way? So now, with our sport in the modern-day world, we jump everything. I mean, we jump the backs of pickup trucks. We jump into water, over ditches, banks, corners, narrow panels. That cross-country part, divided up into several sections, is over fourteen miles. So it has a real endurance side to it.

David O'Connor won the individual gold in eventing at the 2000 Olympics in Sydney.

Barrel Racer Qualifications

To win at the Western sport of barrel racing, you need a fast horse, good riding skills, and razor-sharp timing.

Having qualified for the National Finals Rodeo in four different decades, world champion Martha Josey is the undisputed queen of barrel racing. She also teaches it, and finds that her young students do better if they've already been involved in sports.

> Timing is probably the most important thing in running barrels. You've got to have perfect timing. And you've got to be a thinker. I've always said a good quarterback for a football team could probably be a good barrel racer, too, because they have to think and they've got to outplay their competitor, and you've got to solve problems before they come up. So all of that's real important.

Martha and her husband, world-champion calf roper R.E. Josey, operate the Josey Ranch in Texas. Incidentally, Martha first excelled at basketball.

Super Visualization

One simple technique experts recommend for improving your performance is visualizing the outcome.

People do it all the time. They visualize their goals vividly and begin living into them. Before long the dream becomes reality. Kirsten Farris coaches world-class riders on maximizing their performances through a sort of super-visualization technique that involves not just seeing, but hearing, smelling, feeling, and tasting success. She explains:

> The more of your senses you can pull into visualization, the more believable it is to your brain. And the interesting thing about our brains is that they don't know the difference between imagined and reality.

Positive affirmations play on the same quirk of our brains: the inability to distinguish between images gathered by our senses and those recalled or fabricated in our minds.

Tie-Down Roping

In the rock 'em, sock 'em world of professional rodeo, ropers aren't the only ones doing some spinning.

Calf roping has probably drawn more fire from animal welfare activists than any other rodeo sport. Publicists have attempted to put a different spin on this rapid-fire, timed event by simply changing its name, as author Nancy Jaffer explains.

> There have been cruelty charges leveled against rodeos, so they are very conscious of their image—of taking care of the animals and giving them a good life. They changed the name of calf roping to tie-down roping, because they felt it was more descriptive. But personally, I think they just didn't want the image of a poor little calf being roped.

Calling calf roping tie-down roping hasn't changed the sport, however, and some say that's a good thing. Most animals used in rodeo are valuable commodities, receive the best of care, and live surprisingly long lives.

Racehorse Age

Racing is notorious for the way it stresses young horses, but some get out and have a successful second career.

The typical riding horse is not started under saddle until it is two years old. But by two, the average racehorse is already being run hard and often, a practice that shortens many racing careers. Top racehorse trainer Blane Schvaneveldt has noticed a change in recent years.

> There used to be a lot of horses around here at nine or ten years old, but nowadays, I'd say the average age of a horse around here is five or six years old. They just don't run them as long as they used to. They just seem to go by the wayside. They run 'em hard as twos and threes and fours, and they just don't last, or they're gone doing something else.

That something else could be barrel racing, dressage, eventing, or trail riding. All of these activities are well suited for a good-minded—and sound—retired racehorse.

Team Sorting

Are you a team player? Ready to try an actual sport with your horse? Then team sorting may be just the ticket for you.

Like so many horse sports in the Western riding world, team sorting has its roots in the day-to-day life of the real working cowboy. The object is to move a group of ten cows, numbered one through ten, from one pen to another. The challenge is to move them one at a time, in numerical order. Champion team sorter Roger Braa feels this is a good sport for novice riders.

> It's a little bit slower, so people are more inclined to try it. It really levels the playing field between the pros and the novices because in a small pen like that, you put a little too much pressure—you know how cattle are when you put ten brains in there, all thinking ten different things— anything can happen. I mean, I've been to sortings where novices have won the open.

Team sorting and team penning (its fast-moving, hard-riding cousin) are usually offered at the same events, but they're very different sports.

Order in Eventing

The three different competitions that make up eventing are always conducted in the same order—and for good reason.

No American equestrian is more of an expert on three-day eventing than Olympic gold medalist David O'Connor. He explains why dressage, cross-country, and show jumping are in that order.

> Dressage is your basis of communication, and that should always be first. You should have to prove that you have a level of communication before you're allowed out onto a course where you are going to be riding at speed, at solid obstacles. The cross-country is the meat of our sport, where the event horse proves himself. Then he's got to come out on the third day and prove that he's still useful and that he can do a lot of things.

For a horse to successfully negotiate a show-jumping course after a day of cross-country is like a human athlete playing a competitive round of tennis after running a marathon.

Trick Riding Speed

One of the most thrilling rodeo exhibitions is trick riding, and the faster the horse, the safer the rider.

Like its cousin, the competitive sport of vaulting, trick riding consists of maneuvers done on the back of a moving horse. But that's where the similarity ends. While vaulting utilizes draft horses with broad backs, longed at a slow canter, trick riding is done on lighter, more spirited breeds at a full run in a wide-open arena. Veteran trick rider Lori Jo Orman discusses the necessity of speed:

> You want more speed because it gives you a smoother ride. If you can imagine that a horse, when he runs as fast as he can, his body is more horizontal, and he's stretching out as he covers ground.

Trick riders seem to defy gravity—and death—when they dangle by a foot from the back of a running horse. But one of nature's laws, the law of inertia, keeps them safe.

Extremes in Showing

In the show world, extremes in conformation and way of moving tend to be rewarded, but that may be changing.

Show horse trainers can't make a living unless their horses win, and a horse can't win unless it stands out from the competition. Missouri Fox Trotting Horse trainer Gale Thompson provides this example.

> If you take a foundation-bred Fox Trotting Horse and go out and try to put it in a show ring, you're going to say, "That's a nice Fox Trotting Horse." But it doesn't catch your eye. It doesn't reach out and do something for you. So the trainers are constantly doing things to try and get the judge to really look at that one horse, make him do something just a little different.

But different often means unnatural, even unhealthy, and there's a growing effort throughout the horse industry to discourage the breeding and training practices that make some show horses caricatures of their predecessors.

Racing Sound

When it comes to racing, it's not enough that a horse is sound; he must be *racing sound*, and there's a difference.

It's no secret that racing is one of the most strenuous and dangerous of all equine sports. Sometimes racehorses develop leg problems that make them unsound for racing purposes, but still perfectly acceptable—and a great bargain—for the less-demanding rider. Author Sharon Smith is an expert on retraining horses for new careers.

> You can often find a horse who's got problems in front, and unless you're going to jump, that's okay. On the other hand, you sometimes find horses with problems behind—hock problems—in which case some of the Western sports aren't ideal for them, but you could certainly do trail riding or casual riding or all kinds of other things with them.

Such horses are often called "serviceably sound," and they can go on to have full, useful lives after racing.

Holding Four Reins

Can you imagine controlling the reins for four horses at once? In four-in-hand driving, you do it with one hand!

In four-in-hand driving, you have two pairs of horses pulling a carriage, and there's one rein for each horse. Top driver Chester Weber describes the Achenbach system for controlling all four horses with one hand.

> His system puts the left leader rein on top of your pointer finger on the left hand. Then between your pointer finger and the middle finger, you would have the right leader rein and the left wheeler rein. And then between your ring finger and your middle finger, you would have the right wheeler rein.

The two middle reins are used to keep the carriage going straight; the other reins to make turns. Why do all of this with one hand? Because during the dressage and obstacle course phases of competition, the driver's right hand holds a buggy whip.

Eventing's Third Day

Three-day events are used in both combined training and combined driving competition, but they're not quite the same.

The sport of combined driving is to carriage driving what combined training is to riding. Competition in both centers around three-day events where the first day is a dressage test and the second day is a cross-country race. But while riders face a jumping course on the third day, for drivers it's an obstacle course. America's four-in-hand driving champ, Chester Weber, explains:

> It's basically to show that the horse can come back from having shown the great degree of discipline and elasticity on the first day, and then show the endurance and the vigor and the spirit of the horse on the cross-country day. And it shows that they can again be disciplined and you can drive with a great degree of accuracy and control.

By the age of twenty-six, Chester was already known as one of the world's best drivers.

Training for Cutting Futurity

You'd think that a professional horse trainer would be the safest person to handle a young horse, but that's not always true.

In the high-stakes world of cutting, the first major contest a horse can win is the futurity, and he must do it at the tender age of three, with little more than a year of training. It's a big gamble. Winning a futurity can make a horse a cash cow. But in that year of intensive training, an overzealous trainer could damage the youngster, as legendary cutter Leon Harrel knows all too well.

> It's when they get to pushing and asking too much, too quick on those colts when they're too young, and maybe they don't have adequate time for the training schedule. Language breaks down with them, leadership falls to the side, and first thing you know, they wind up crippling a colt.

One solution that has been proposed is to make this key contest for older colts—four- or even five-year-olds. That would allow a horse to be trained for the futurity with less risk of gambling his future away.

Setting Goals in Showing

If you're going to reach your big goals, the experts say you've got to set smaller goals along the way.

All productive activity requires goal setting as a way of motivating, directing, and measuring your efforts. Sports consultant Kirsten Farris coaches world champion–level riders, and she says you need three different types of goals.

> The *outcome* goal is kind of your big, dream goal, which happens about twelve months out. And then what you want to do is break that up into what we call *process* goals, which are really the milestones. And then *performance* goals, which really help you determine what you need to do in order to reach your process goal.

If your outcome goal is winning a world championship, one process goal might be getting qualified to go to the world show, and one performance goal might be to always nail your lead changes.

Heavy on the Forehand

In the show world, a horse that is heavy on the forehand is not likely to win any trophies or buckles.

A horse's power comes from his hind end. Before he can propel himself forward, he must get his hind legs under his body, and shift his weight back. In the show world, this is called *collection*, and it takes some work to get a horse to carry himself this way, basically because he's not built to do it. Dressage champion Lendon Gray explains why:

> He's got this big head and big neck in front of his front feet, and then just the body between his front legs and his hind legs. So because of the way God designed him, he's got more weight on his front end. We need to encourage the horse, over a period of time, to learn to shift his weight back, to be better balanced for the job, whatever the job may be.

But being front-heavy isn't a cosmic mistake. It helps balance the horse during two of his favorite pastimes: grazing and dozing.

Voice Aids in Dressage

The rules governing dressage tests do not allow voice aids, but riders find ways to get around that.

Dressage has its origins in the military, and that sort of commitment to following the rules is still very much a part of the sport. According to British trainer Tanya Larrigan, even though voice aids are forbidden, dressage riders from many countries still use them, even at the risk of being penalized.

> You'd lose two points every time you did it, but you become a very good ventriloquist. You find each country tends to have some special noise it might use for a slow down or a steady. If I'm doing an extended gallop, I personally would say "whoa" as I'm coming back at the end of the diagonal. That just sets him up and he knows straight away that the other aid's going to follow.

Note that the voice is not used instead of a traditional aid, but in addition to it—kind of like saying, "Get ready! Something important is coming."

The Evolution of Halter Horses

They say that life is too short to ride an ugly horse, but some of the most beautiful horses can't even be ridden.

Like bodybuilding contests, halter or model classes tend to favor horses with exaggerated conformation. In the Quarter Horse breed, halter champions are usually very large and heavily muscled. They have disproportionately small feet and they're almost never ridden. Legendary showman Al Dunning longs for the good old days.

> We used to have a functional horse that could show in the reining, show in the roping, and then show at halter and win all of them. When I was a kid growing up, if you won the aged mare class, or the aged stud class, the chances of you winning the Western pleasure were about 98 percent. And nowadays, if you've won one of the halter classes, chances of you *not* being in the performance is about 100 percent.

Don't expect major changes any time soon. Halter horses today are big business.

Refusing a Jump

It is probably the greatest fear that the typical rider has in a jumping class—his horse refusing a jump.

A refused jump can send a rider rocketing off his horse and into a serious injury. Fortunately, the horse often signals his intent with a subtle lessening of his forward momentum and a slight shifting back of his weight. The experienced rider feels this and instantly drives the horse forward with first leg pressure, then spur, then riding stick, if needed. Hunter/jumper clinician Anna Jane White-Mullin elaborates:

> When the horse is coming to the fence, the first time it crosses his mind, "You know, maybe I'll just stop on this gal"—if you go with the stick, it's the perception that you're onto the horse. He says, "Well, this isn't worth doing because she knows where I'm going with this."

It was a refused jump on a cross-country course that caused the spinal cord injury and eventual death of popular actor Christopher Reeve.

Somatic Anxiety

Can your horse actually read your mind? Then how else would he know when you're nervous about performing?

Sports psychologists have a name for the butterflies you get before performing. They call it *somatic anxiety*, and there are physical manifestations of it. Showing consultant Kirsten Farris describes the symptoms:

> Your body gets tight, your breathing gets rapid, and your palms get sweaty. Yet mentally you don't notice that you're anxious. It doesn't really register. Your horse feels that somatic anxiety. When your horse maybe starts kind of chewing on his bit, or digs a little, things like that—they feel that bit of tenseness.

Kirsten teaches riders to relax their muscles by relaxing their bodies first, then their minds. Interestingly, instead of breathing rapidly, some riders literally forget to breathe. The horse picks that up instantly and interprets it as meaning danger is at hand.

Weighted Horseshoes

In the world of fancy show horses, the quality of shoeing can mean the difference between winning and losing.

At American Saddlebred shows, the high-stepping, super-animated horse will garner the most praise from judges and audiences alike. But how do you get a horse to do something like that? According to Saddlebred judge and trainer Gayle Lampe, one key is the careful use of weighted horseshoes.

> Some trainers who are not very qualified might think more is better, but that is definitely not true. Each horse will tell you how much weight he can comfortably carry and still do his gaits properly and stay sound. And the Saddlebred horse has to be sound because he trots. If a horse is lame when he trots, then he is absolutely not competitive.

The weighted shoes require extra effort to lift and tend to exaggerate the horse's movement, which is the whole point in this kind of competition.

Preperformance Rituals

Preperformance rituals may help quiet your mind and get you ready to compete, but what do they mean to your horse?

Watch a basketball player prepare to shoot a free throw, a batter as he readies himself for the pitch, or a sprinter settling himself in the starting blocks. They all have rituals, routines performed the same way every time, to get their minds focused on the task at hand. Good riders do the same thing when they compete, and it produces the same benefit for them—but how does the horse take all this? Equestrian performance consultant Kirsten Farris provides some insight:

> A secondary benefit is that the horse picks up on that. We all know that our horses get used to certain patterns and rituals, and so they understand, "Okay, now we're going to compete." And so, it gets you ready as a team, and the more you communicate with your horse, the more you can help get your horse ready; the more relaxed you are, the better your horse is going to be.

Learning from Losing

World champion and Olympic riders often have more experience with the disappointment of losing than the thrill of winning. It's character, determination, and the will to succeed that gives them the strength to persevere and eventually win. So how do they deal with losing along the way? Many, like gold medalist David O'Connor, choose to look at the positive side of losing.

> When you have a really bad competition, because of your own personal performance or because of what you thought was going to happen, that is when you learn. You learn more about your technique or who you are, what your competitive values are, and where you need to do some work. So, you learn a lot more off of the disappointments than you do off the wins.

And there's another downside to winning: You can only go downhill from there. Your own success can be a hard act to follow.

Pinwheel Maneuver

A drill team is a fun way to do something competitive with your horse, but beware the mighty pinwheel.

Many of us were in marching band in high school and remember how hard it was to keep a straight line. Equestrian drill teams have an even tougher task—especially when they attempt the pinwheel maneuver, says drill team expert Wayne Williams.

> The outside horse sets the pace on how fast you're bringing it around, and all the horses in the middle of that line have to continually adjust between the outside and inside horse. They are always looking whether they have to speed up or slow down, and if anybody tries to adjust the pace, other than the outside horse, you're going to get a line that looks pretty crooked. The inside pivots at whatever rate they can, but the outside horse is what's setting the pace on that.

Ideally, the inside horse should be simply rotating in place. Depending on the number of horses and size of the pinwheel, the outside horse may be galloping full out.

Stretching and Collection

In riding, nothing is more beautiful than a nicely collected horse, and the secret to getting that is stretching him out.

Weight training, running, swimming, tennis, softball—we're taught that before engaging in any of these strenuous activities, we need to do stretching exercises. They help prepare our muscles and reduce the chance of injury. The most strenuous thing we ask a horse to do is perform maneuvers in a collected frame with a rider on his back. Yet most of us don't think about stretching him out first, according to dressage clinician and author Mike Schaffer.

> Everybody now is confused about it, but all the old masters of dressage knew darn well that the way you get a horse to compress his frame is to teach him to first stretch out his frame. And when he first stretches out his frame, and builds his muscles and gets in the habit of getting his hind legs underneath him, then he lifts his back and elevates the frame in front by himself.

Saddle-Seat Hand Technique

If you're accustomed to riding Western, hunt seat, or even dressage, saddle-seat riding is just plain weird.

When you're showing your horse in Western classes, your elbow should be bent slightly, with your hands angled toward the ground. Hunt-seat hand position is similar, but without the bend at the elbow. Saddle seat is completely different. Trainer Gayle Lampe explains:

> We totally break up that straight line. We have our elbows down and our lower arm can be higher—in many cases, *is* higher—than the elbow. So the wrist and the hands are going to be higher than the elbow. And when you bump back in the saddle-seat style of riding, you don't pull back toward your waist. You bump up with quick little vibrating nips on the horse's mouth. But you bump up toward the rafters or up toward the sky.

Saddle seat is meant to be flashy and animated. It's what judges and audiences look for, and once you see it, you probably won't forget it.

Walking a Cross-Country Course

If you think you're a pretty good rider and want to step up to the big leagues, try three-day eventing—but beware of day two.

Day two of three-day eventing competitions is more grueling and dangerous than days one or three. Known as the cross-country day, it tests the stamina of horse and rider, and consists of four phases: Short Roads and Tracks, Steeplechase, Long Roads and Tracks, and Cross-Country. David O'Connor, gold medalist at the 2000 Olympics in Sydney, talks about how he prepares for day two.

> The riders are given a couple days to walk it, so you know every inch of ground, where you're going to change speeds, what lines you're going to take. I'm going to show this fence so that my horse can see it the soonest. Those are all the things that you've got to plan to make it work well.

There are no practice runs, and no matter how well the rider knows the course, the horse is seeing it for the first time and must temper his exuberance and speed with total obedience to the rider's commands.

Leaning on the Bit

Racing is a horse of a different color, and nowhere is that more evident than in the way the bit is used.

For showing and recreational riding, you don't want your horse leaning on his bit. It puts his weight too far forward, makes steering him more difficult, and wears out the rider's arms. But in horse racing, where all that matters is speed, leaning on the bit is desirable and horses are trained to do it, as racehorse trainer and author Janet Del Castillo describes:

> We don't do a racehorse a favor if we're light on his mouth. We want to teach him to lean into the bit. By holding that bit and giving him very firm guidance, we're helping him along. You will see that at the end of the race, where maybe the horse wants to quit and the jockey just keeps driving on him and he holds that head up and keeps that horse going.

Photos shot at the finish line show jockeys pulling back on their horses' reins as they reach for the wire. It's not to slow them down, but to speed them up.

Senior Endurance Riders

So many sports are geared toward young people, but endurance riding is attracting its share of older riders.

In her biography *Ten Feet Tall, Still*, veteran endurance rider Julie Suhr tells of a life dedicated to this demanding sport. For Julie, there's no retirement in sight, as evidenced by her recent participation in an especially grueling California ride with her husband, Bob.

> There is a 200-mile endurance ride over a course of four days between Christmas and New Year's down in the Death Valley area. We went through two feet of snow at 7,500 feet, and then we dropped back down to almost the valley floor. Bob chose to ride one day, which was the first day, and he completed it very nicely with a horse fit to continue, which is the criteria we use for endurance riding.

Riding fifty miles in one day is an accomplishment at any age. By the way, at the time of this ride, Julie was seventy-nine and Bob was eighty-four.

Higher Action

High-headed and high-stepping, English show horses look like they're trying to climb a ladder into the sky.

Throughout history, statues of famous generals on their horses have depicted mounts with high action. It had a practical benefit: an elevated front end made quick changes of direction possible. Just as important, high action was considered fancy, and everyone, from generals to the general public, admired a fancy horse. Saddle-seat expert Gayle Lampe provides more detail:

> People wanted to show off their means of transportation, which is what these horses were back then, and if your horse had a higher head carriage, wore that overcheck better, and could get his knee up higher and bend his hocks a little bit more, he was fancier than your neighbor's horse. And then they started having competitions; in addition to racing competitions, they had show competitions.

Today this is known as saddle-seat riding, and it's dominated by the American Saddlebred.

Good Endurance Horses

The stress and strain of endurance riding requires a horse with exceptional physical and mental strength.

Some horses are better suited than others to the rigors of fifty- and hundred-mile endurance rides. According to endurance riding legend, Julie Suhr, pasture-raised horses are more likely than stall-raised horses to have the natural athleticism needed. But there's another factor that's just as important:

> The mind of the horse, the attitude of the horse. You want to ride a horse that when you are at the bottom of a mountain and you look up and you think, "I want to get to the top of that mountain," that horse wants to get up there as much as you do. And then, if you get one with the physical ability, you have really got a champion horse.

Arabian horses dominate the sport of endurance riding, primarily because of their exceptional stamina, but individuals of various breeds, including smooth-riding gaited horses, have also been used successfully.

Best Condition Award

In most races, he who finishes first wins, but there's one sport where number ten may take home the greatest glory.

The lay press has called it an extreme sport, and has suggested that it's abusive to horses. But endurance racing could be the most humane of all riding disciplines. There are vet checks at regular intervals during each race, and the horse's condition at the end of the race is of supreme importance. Endurance champ Julie Suhr elaborates:

> They take the first ten horses to cross the finish line. They then have the veterinarians go over those ten horses carefully and decide which one is in the best condition, and they get a Best Condition award; that's a very desirable award and sometimes held in higher esteem than the first-place award. And what it proves is that you've ridden that horse and he's finished the ride in better shape than the others.

Races range up to one hundred miles, and riders are often competitive into their seventies. Now that's good condition!

Drug-Free Endurance

As demanding as endurance racing is on horses, what's even more demanding is the monitoring of each horse's condition.

No sport puts greater importance on avoiding injury to its horses than endurance racing. Mandatory rest stops and veterinary checks sometimes add hours to a rider's time in the interest of keeping the horse sound. Veteran endurance champion Julie Suhr offers another example of the sport's commitment to the horse's welfare.

> We are also a drug-free sport. Our horses are not allowed to have any anti-inflammatories in them or any painkillers whatsoever, and the horses are tested at random. So horses are out there going on their own ability with no pharmaceutical things to help.

In some horse sports, anti-inflammatory injections are given at the first sign of discomfort in a horse. But masking pain would go against everything held sacred in the sport of endurance riding.

Claiming Race

In horse racing, the claiming race is an ingenious way of keeping horses as evenly matched as possible.

Outspoken racehorse trainer Janet Del Castillo is the author of *Backyard Racehorse*. She explains how a claiming race works.

> For example, a $5,000 claiming price would mean the horse is worth $5,000 in that race. So any horse, regardless of what he cost and all the thousands you have put into him, is entered in this race where another owner or trainer fifteen minutes before the race may put in a slip and claim him. They own it at the point when the gates open.

The old owner gets the money from the sale and any purse winnings. The new owner gets the horse. Claiming races are designed to regulate the level of competition because they discourage entering a horse above or below his ability. Incidentally, only trainers and owners properly licensed by the racetrack are eligible to claim horses there.

Drill Team Origins

As a fighting force, the U.S. Cavalry no longer exists, but its riding maneuvers are the basis of a popular sport.

Drill teams present an opportunity for riders of all ages and abilities to take part in a competitive team sport with their horses. Horse expo promoter and announcer Wayne Williams is a thirty-year veteran of drill teams. He talks about their military roots:

> When you moved the cavalry, whether you were moving in lines of two or lines of four, you had to effectively be able to turn that cavalry around. So you would do it just like if you were marching in the military: Do a column right or a column left or a twos or fours right, twos or fours left. All of the old horse-soldier maneuvers were the basis of these drill teams.

Modern drill team routines contain plenty of new moves, too. In fact, although they are still used for warm-ups, the original horse-soldier battle maneuvers form a very small part of the repertoire you see in competition.

Old Saddle-Seat Posture

It's not English and it's certainly not Western. In fact, saddle-seat equitation isn't even what it used to be.

Nearly all riding today is done using the classic riding posture, with shoulders, hips, and heels in vertical alignment. But saddle seat, the style of riding used with high-stepping show horses, hasn't always been that way, says saddle-seat trainer and judge, Gayle Lampe.

> The old-fashioned way of riding saddle seat was, you kind of put the rider in the chair seat with your legs out in front of you, and the old plantation riders, when they used to go check the fence back in the old days, they would sit down and have their legs out in front of them. We have totally gotten away from that. Our leg position really is pretty much the same as the stock-seat rider.

Saddle-seat classes are offered for Saddlebreds, Arabians, National Show Horses, Morgans, and even Friesians and Andalusians—but so far, no stock horses.

 **Jump-Off**

To win in the competitive world of jumping, you need to be smart, fast, and fearless, but not all at the same time.

Jumping classes in horse shows have two phases. Phase one is all about control. You must clear every jump in the course cleanly within the allotted time. Those who are successful are invited back for phase two, the jump-off, where boldness must be added to the mix. Hunter/jumper instructor Lori Cramer explains:

> Let's say there was a bending line and there were six strides in it; you would go direct in five in the jump-off. Not necessarily faster, but take the bend out of the line to make your time better. So you can see, there are all different options. There'll be inside turns versus outside turns, and the person that has not just the fastest time but makes the wisest choices is going to be the winner of that class. Sometimes you go too fast and you miss the turn. That's not helpful.

For the jump-off, the pattern through the course is often changed, adding another thing to think about.

Too Much Practice

If you want to excel at showing horses, you have to practice; but is it possible to practice too much?

Whether it's music or dance or sports or riding horses, it's rare for children to practice as much as they should. There are just too many other things going on in their busy young lives. But occasionally, whether from parental pressure or a child's own drive to succeed, the child will become compulsive about improving his skills. That isn't always good for the horses involved, as hunter/jumper instructor Louise Serio explains.

> They get kind of sour; they get average. You might have a real top-quality horse, but if you just keep jumping and jumping and jumping, you'll have an average horse. So, it's really about balancing how much can the horse take today? How much does the child need? What are we going to do to keep everybody at their peak?

In a perfect world, horse and rider would peak just before the event they're training for.

Barrels for Beginners

One of the most exciting Western riding sports is barrel racing, and you need the right horse to get started.

Veteran barrel racer Martha Josey has qualified for the National Finals Rodeo in four different decades, and is still winning major competitions. Her advice for anyone starting barrel racing is to get an experienced, older horse.

> The best barrel racing horse for a beginner has to be a teenage horse, one that's already been there, done that. He's got some age, he's very well-patterned. He doesn't have to have the most speed in the world, but he's got to be consistent, and he's got to be safe.

Martha and her husband, world-champion calf roper R.E. Josey, operate the Josey Ranch in Karnack, Texas, and focus on teaching riding and roping to young riders of all ages.

CHAPTER FIVE

Equipment

Poly Rope

A cowboy's rope used to be woven from organic material like rawhide or grass. Not anymore.

World-champion calf roper R.E. Josey is spending his golden years teaching youngsters the skills that made him famous. R.E. is a big fan of modern poly ropes because of their feel, which is consistent, regardless of the weather.

> The old grass ropes, you had to either put them under your car hood and warm them up to get the moisture out, or you had to put water in your rope can to keep them picked up, so it was always a hassle. But the poly rope is the same all the time, so these kiddos can get one rope—and they last good, too.

Poly ropes come in different thicknesses, with different degrees of stiffness, and with the coils laid for left-handed or right-handed ropers. Though not affected by weather, a good poly rope is an investment, and serious ropers keep theirs in carrying bags when not in use.

Reining Arena Base

Ever wonder why top reining horses can do such long sliding stops? It's part horse, part human, and part dirt.

To win at the Western riding sport of reining, you've got to have a great stop, and you need a certain kind of arena footing to best demonstrate that. It all starts with the base, the part of the footing you can't see. Arena specialist Bob Kiser reveals his recipe.

> What I like is about a 50 percent sand, 50 percent clay mixture, which has to be a compacted material so you have a smooth, level surface. That's done, of course, for a reining horse, so he can do sliding stops. And then your top material contains more sand so it will stay a little looser.

That loose topping above the base is typically about two and a half inches deep and is a mixture of 80 percent sand and 20 percent clays and silts—what you and I would call good, clean dirt.

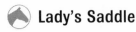 **Lady's Saddle**

Saddlemaking has long focused on fitting the male body. Now, ladies, there are saddles built with your bodies in mind.

Astute saddlemakers like Oregon's Jeremiah Johnson know that the female pelvis has a different tilt when it's in a neutral position than does the male pelvis. Guys tend to slouch and gals don't. Just watch any mixed group of riders relaxing on their horses and you'll see the difference. And according to Jeremiah, the tilt of the pelvis is not the only difference to take into account in a lady's saddle.

> You also have the width across your ground seat. Women have more tissue inside their legs. By nature, men have more of an oval-shaped thigh; women have a round-shaped thigh, so you have to make your ground seats narrower underneath their thighs to incorporate that.

Jeremiah will make a saddle exclusively for a male or female rider, but as a practical matter, he more often "splits the difference" to produce a seat that will be comfortable for any rider.

🐎 Use of a Flag

A flag is usually symbolic of a group of people, but flags can also communicate in more active ways.

Semaphore flags have long been used by the navy for visual communication over short distances. Horse trainers also communicate with flags, although they take quite a different form. Round pen trainer Vaughn Knudsen describes the flag he uses when working with unbroke horses.

> It's a PVC pipe, about ten feet long, maybe two inches in diameter, with a plastic bag tied on the end of it. And what it does, it allows me to extend myself to the horse, so if the horse strikes or kicks out at me, I'm at a safe distance.

The flag is used to desensitize the horse to being touched all over his body. It can also be used to sensitize him to pressure, either tactile or visual, and teach him to move away from it, all the while keeping the trainer at a safe distance.

 **Snaffle Bit**

To the uninitiated it has a funny-sounding name, but the snaffle bit is an important tool in training horses.

The snaffle is the mildest form of bit, and offers the rider the most direct control over the horse's mouth. It's used in English riding, in racing, in driving, and in starting the training of nearly all horses. Clinician Richard Shrake describes this key piece of equipment:

> It's a bit that goes directly from your hands to his mouth. Now, it can be a broken mouthpiece; it can be a straight mouthpiece. It can be anything, but there is no leverage, and that's the true definition of a snaffle. Now, we can work on the right side; we can work on the left side, because all horses are in two. With a snaffle, it's a one-on-one.

After his initial training, the Western riding horse has traditionally been switched to a leverage or curb bit, but that's no longer a given. Today, he just might stay in a snaffle.

Wade Saddle

For decades, the Wade-style saddle has been a favorite among working cowboys and students of horsemanship.

With its slick fork, deep seat, and high cantle, the Wade has the basic look of an old-time cowboy saddle, except for the way it sits on the horse. A wider gullet allows the front end to ride lower, a design feature more commonly seen in English saddles, but one that makes mounting and roping easier on the horse's back. Ranch horse clinician Curt Pate elaborates:

> An English saddle sits a lot closer in the gullet than a Western saddle. The higher up your saddle is, the more torque, and so by getting that saddle down lower in the front end, the less pull and torque there is on that saddle horn.

Born around 1889, Cliff Wade left us with more than a useful saddle design. He was an important influence on the man generally considered the father of natural horsemanship, Tom Dorrance.

Snakebite Kit

You're out on the trail and are bitten by a snake. The first thing to do is forget your old Boy Scout training.

For generations, anyone venturing into the backcountry was advised to carry a snakebite kit with a razor blade, tourniquet, and suction cup. The rather gruesome treatment recommended had a certain logic to it. Problem was, it didn't work, says Dr. Ken Marcella.

> As far as making an X and cutting into the tissue, that's no longer recommended. The damage that you do to tissues and the additional bleeding to that site further distributes the toxin. You should never suck any venom out by mouth. It is very toxic, and you could ingest it and end up with problems there. Now, if you have a suction cup in the kit, you can suck whatever you can from that particular area. It has not proven to be very beneficial, but it gives you something to do.

To be prepared for snakebite, today's trail rider is advised to take along an instant cold pack, a cell phone, and a friend.

Tapping a Horse

Modern horsemanship has brought with it some new applications for traditional tools like the whip.

Just the name conjures up images of brutality. But even in days past, the whip wasn't always used to inflict pain upon a horse; it could also be a more subtle communication device, as French trainer J.P. Giacomini explains.

> Touch somebody with a whip with any kind of energy, and it's sharp. It stings. And if it stings, it gives adrenaline. Somebody comes behind you by surprise and gives you two or three friendly little taps, you're not going to turn around ready to punch them. You're going to say, "Oh. Who is that? What do you want?" The horse does the same thing.

J.P. uses a device he has named the Endo-Stick, which has a handle like a whip, but a foam rubber ball instead of a lash on the end. He rhythmically taps the horse with his Endo-Stick to calm the horse and put it in a learning frame of mind.

Combined Driving Carriages

Combined driving could be the most challenging of all equine sports, and one of the most expensive for its participants.

Combined driving competition is in the form of three-day events. Day one is a dressage test, day two is a cross–country marathon, and day three is an obstacle course. The carriages alone cost tens of thousands of dollars, and you need two different kinds to compete, as America's top four-in-hand driver, Chester Weber, explains.

> On the first and the last day, it's more of an older, more traditional-looking carriage that somebody would have driven to town or whatever, with four horses. And then on the second day, the marathon carriage is really very modern. It's all made of steel, with disk brakes off of a car.

Add in the cost of five or six warmblood horses, feed, and international travel for all of this, and you begin to understand why sponsorship is so important in this sport.

Saddle Bums

Most casual riders get saddle-sore after just a couple of hours in the saddle. Fortunately, there's a solution.

Californian Stan Dill loves to ride, but he had a problem that took most of the joy out of it: Stan got saddle-sore—so sore that he would bleed after less than an hour in the saddle. Drawing on his background in the textile business, Stan invented riding underwear that takes the trauma out of trail riding. He calls them Saddle Bums, and here's why they work.

> The outer shell is slippery so that it can move underneath your jeans. Inside of that, there are two different types of pads—one for men, one for women—designed to actually wick the moisture away from your skin through the shell, and eventually, out through your jeans. I can actually ride for eight or ten hours without getting saddle-sore.

Saddle Bums virtually eliminate heat and friction, the main causes of saddle-soreness.

Slick Fork and Slick Seat

Look at the saddles of working cowboys and you'll find most of them are pretty slick—in more ways than one.

For ranch work, the traditional buckaroo-style saddle remains popular. It has a higher cantle, larger horn, and a slick fork—in other words, no swells built into the pommel. Such saddles also have a slick, unpadded seat, which is actually more comfortable on long rides. Saddle Bums founder Stan Dill elaborates:

> People call me that are going to guest ranches, and they're going on an elk hunt or one of these things, and they're not an experienced rider. I recommend a saddle that has a slick seat, because, particularly with a Western saddle, you need to roll with the horse. You need to slide, and if you're protected with our garment, and you can slide in the saddle, you're going to have a successful trip.

Stan invented Saddle Bums, padded riding underwear that even rugged cowboys now use to protect their tender tushes.

World Show Arena

When you're sitting in the stands watching world show classes, you don't think about the arena footing, but the riders sure do.

Just as horses today are bred and trained with specialized purposes in mind, the arenas where top-level competitions take place are also purpose-built. But at the American Quarter Horse Association World Show, all classes must share the same arena, where only minor variations in the footing are possible. Arena specialist Bob Kiser discusses the difficulty of this task:

> It is a challenge to find the right material there, because you go from cutting to reining. With cutting, they want that footing pretty deep and pretty loose, and then with the reining, you've got to establish a base in that same material.

To make the best of it, reining is never scheduled right after cutting; there are always several classes in between, providing more opportunities for Bob's crew to work on the base before reiners begin their spinning and sliding.

Tongue Release

Have you ever wondered why so many bits have a rise—or port—in the middle of the mouthpiece? It's for tongue release.

Curb bits are all about giving the rider leverage on the horse's head. Contrary to what you might think, the port or rise in the bit's mouthpiece makes the action milder, because it takes pressure off the tongue. Veteran show horse trainer Richard Shrake explains why this is important.

> When we have a lot of tongue release, it means that the signal then goes more out to the corners of the lips. When our signal is to the corner of the lips, he's going to be a little lighter. There are some horses that have had a cut tongue, so we want to get the pressure off of it. That bothers us. There are some horses with a real short, thick tongue that can't take any pressure on it, so a lot of tongue release helps with that.

Proper adjustment of the curb strap under the horse's chin keeps the port from hurting the roof of the horse's mouth.

Rigging Position

The rigging position on a Western saddle determines where on the horse's back the saddle will ride.

If the front cinch on a Western saddle attaches directly under the fork, the saddle's rigging is in the *full* position, and the rider sits farther back. If halfway between the pommel and the cantle, it's a *center-fire* rigging, and the rider is positioned more forward on the horse. In between are the more common options, *three-quarters* and *seven-eighths*. Ranch horse clinician Curt Pate explains his choice.

> To me, the most balanced part of the horse is the fourteenth vertebra, and that's right behind the withers. So the closer we can get to the withers of the horse, the better—and that's why my rigging position on my saddle is a three-quarter rig. The rigging is where your cinch hangs down. The farther back it is, the farther it sets me forward toward that fourteenth vertebra, and then I think I don't mess up the balance of my horse near as much as if I'm sitting way back.

Severity of the Bit

Bits come in varying degrees of severity, and that has a direct bearing on how they should be used.

What makes a bit mild or severe? The way the rider uses it, of course. But the design of the bit matters, too. A thicker mouthpiece is milder. A thinner one is more severe. Veteran horseman Richard Shrake points out another factor: the surface texture.

> A smooth surface is very mild. A surface that has a twist, a rough surface, is like a chain saw. Those little teeth on there can actually take the soft tissue in that horse's mouth, and tear a little bit of that right out of him, if your hands are quick and your hands are bad.

In general, a curb bit, which gives the rider leverage on the horse's mouth, is more severe than a snaffle bit, which has a direct, unleveraged connection. But the real issue is the rider's hands—how heavy or light they are.

Chicago Screw in a Bridle

The Chicago screw may be perfect for a lot of applications, but not for holding a bridle together.

Sometimes so-called improvements to the tools we depend on are really just changes to make manufacturing easier and more profitable. Such is probably the case with Chicago screws being used to hold bridles together. Clinician Charles Wilhelm would agree.

> A Chicago screw is like a barrel that has threads, and then the bolt kind of screws into it; this way, it's both finished and rounded so it doesn't hurt the horse. But with vibration and use, they back out, and then the bridle is left dangling. I really don't care for Chicago screws. I've lost them myself out on the trail; you lose the bit, and then you're in a real predicament.

What's better than a Chicago screw in a bridle? How about something so simple and ancient that it was probably used on the very first bridle? Leather string.

Copper in a Bit

Most bits sold for horses today are stainless steel. But you'll often see a roller or other component of the mouthpiece that's made of copper. Trainer, judge, and bit expert Richard Shrake explains why:

> Copper in a mix gets the horse to lick it, and it creates a little saliva. But you never saw the old masters make a bit with solid copper. It always had a mix, because the solid copper by itself is way too hot, and then he chomps it rather than licks it.

By itself, copper is too soft for a bit anyway. But a nickel and copper alloy has been developed that seems ideal for bit manufacture. And without the characteristic reddish cast, it passes at horse shows for normal stainless steel.

Ansür Treeless Saddle

Since the saddle's inception, a rigid tree has always been an integral part of the design—but not anymore.

When a horse moves, the shape of his back changes. Grand Prix dressage rider Peter DeCosemo believes the saddle should change, too, so he invented the treeless Ansür saddle, to the ridicule and bewilderment of an industry steeped in tradition.

> They can't figure out how we actually do it, without a rigid framework to stretch all of the leatherwork over, and with nothing to nail it and staple it to; and then we put the padding in. Most of the saddlemakers just have no idea how we do it.

The Ansür saddle is built up in multiple layers, starting with a core of stiff latigo leather, and incorporating space-age cushioning material, like that used in football pads. The result is a traditional-looking English saddle with the ability to flex with the horse's movement. The Ansür saddle gets high marks from riders and horses alike.

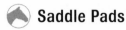 Saddle Pads

You say you don't want to buy a new custom saddle every time you change horses? A good saddle pad may be the answer.

Poor saddle fit can make even the gentlest horse irritable and dangerous to its rider. But the right saddle pad can sometimes make the fit a whole lot better. Riding instructor Julie Goodnight offers this example:

> If you go from a horse with low withers to a horse with high withers, you can get a split-withered pad for the high-withered horse. So to a degree, you can have some flexibility. We have a number of school horses here in all shapes and sizes, and we switch saddles around a lot depending on the size of the rider.

Saddle pads are available today with space-age cushioning materials. You can also get gel-filled or air-filled pads that mold themselves to the contours of the horse's back and the bottom of the saddle.

In-Skirt Rigging

Can you imagine competing in a track meet wearing a corset? That's the effect some Western saddles have on horses.

The rigging system of a saddle provides a means of attaching the cinch straps that hold the saddle on. Traditional rigging designs provide D-rings that are connected to the saddle's tree via straps passing under the saddle's skirt. Some newer designs are quite different in their rigging, and according to saddlemaker David Genadek, newer is not always better.

> What we're doing on a lot of saddles is, we're taking that D-ring and we're putting it in the skirt, so when we cinch up our saddle the whole skirt is wrapping around the shoulder and acting like a girdle, causing a lot of restriction. We started doing this after we stopped using rear cinches.

With no rear cinch, the back of the saddle tended to flop up and down. Better saddles today still use traditional rigging and have both front and back cinches.

Burr on a Bit

Two bits of the same brand and style are going to be the same, right? Wrong—and it could affect your horse's behavior.

Bitmakers are often not horsemen. They don't understand how sensitive a horse's mouth is. A horse will tolerate a bump, burr, or other manufacturing irregularity in a bit, but not for very long. If your horse starts tossing his head or wanting to run off with you half an hour into your ride, it's possible he's just run out of patience with his bit. Popular clinician Richard Shrake offers this analogy.

> Have you ever had a little piece of spinach in your tooth? About in the middle of the night you wake up and run and get a toothpick, don't you? Well, a horse is the same way, only the horse doesn't have the luxury of running and grabbing a toothpick. You put the bridle on, he's got to live with it.

Bite marks can also render a good bit unusable, so to be safe, check your horse's bit for rough spots every time you use it.

Trick-Riding Saddles

An important tool of the trick rider's trade is the saddle, and it's a little different than a normal saddle.

Performing breathtaking maneuvers on the back of a running horse is all in a day's work for a rodeo trick rider. And one reason you really shouldn't try this at home is the special saddle these equestrian gymnasts use. Trick rider Lori Jo Orman explains:

> They look similar to a Western saddle, except the horn that we have is often six to eight inches long. It would look like a baton from a twirler out of a marching band. We also have handholds on the back called cruppers, and each saddle is customized to the particular trick rider.

Trick-riding saddles may look funny, but they're all business. Trick riders trust their lives to them every time they enter the arena to perform.

Reining Arena Footing

It may look like a school playground, but a reining arena is a precise blend of sand and, well . . . dirt.

The basic footing in almost any riding arena is sand, but it is often supplemented with other materials. Crumb rubber is a popular additive for jumping arenas. Wood chips are mixed with sand in dressage arenas, and for reining, arena specialist Bob Kiser prefers something different still:

> The sand that I use on top is a little bit different than most dressage arenas or some other horse arenas. I use a sand with a percentage of silts and clays in it, normally around a 20 percent.

Bob, buddy, that's dirt—although I agree it *is* fancy dirt. By the way, sand alone tends to be too slippery for reining. The silts and clays give the footing added stability, leading to better performances and fewer injuries.

CHAPTER SIX

Care

Grass in Nature

For horses in the wild, grass is one of the most important natural resources. Let's find out how it works.

As with most things in nature, grass has a natural cycle and will flourish, even when being periodically devoured by herbivores like the horse. Pasture management guru Bryan Pulliam elaborates:

> A herd of horses will move fifteen to twenty miles per day, always onto new grass. Herds of buffalo will swarm through an area, trampling the ground and devastating the grasses for one day—but then they're gone. Then the grass has several weeks to regrow. This is nature. One day grazing to several weeks of rest.

The recovery period for grass allows its leaves to grow above the ground and its roots to grow below. According to Bryan, the leaves must grow back six to eight inches in order for the plant to feed itself using photosynthesis.

Grazing on Small Pasture

Anyone who knows horses will tell you that grazing is the most natural way of feeding them. But take heart. Full-time turnout doesn't require the holdings of a land baron. Pasture management expert Bryan Pulliam explains.

Five full-grown horses, moving into six- to eight-inch grass, will need only one-tenth of an acre—or approximately sixty by seventy feet of new grass—to consume for the day. Most people think in terms of two and three acres per paddock. We actually think in terms of sixty by seventy feet for five full-grown horses.

So if you allow grass four weeks to re-grow after a day of grazing, five horses could be supported full-time on a total of just three acres of good pasture! This "intensive rotational grazing" requires subdividing your pasture into many small paddocks, and moving your horses to a new one daily.

Pasture Lanes

Horses are meant to graze and move continually throughout the day. How can we emulate that in a small pasture?

The challenge of providing natural management of horses on small acreages has led to some creative solutions. Rancher Bryan Pulliam divides his pasture into small paddocks and can thereby move his horses to new grass every day. That meets the need for grazing, but what about movement? Horses in nature often walk fifteen or more miles a day! Bryan has planned for that, too.

> We like to have our horses be able to move maybe a quarter mile to a half a mile, at will, through some contained lanes and corridors. Those are throwaway areas because they're trampled and they don't maintain good grass, but that's a very small amount of land. The movement of the horses is no problem.

Why would the horses use these lanes? Because they connect that day's grazing area to the central, permanent drinking area.

Self-Cleaning Pasture

The self-cleaning pasture is here, thanks not to scientific invention, but to Mother Nature and a common insect.

There's one thing every horse owner must come to grips with: Horses produce lots of manure, or dung. Cleaning stalls is one thing, but what about pastures? Rancher Bryan Pulliam introduces the horseman's friend, the dung beetle.

> There are many, many types: Some will live in the dung. Some will burrow immediately below the dung. Some will travel fifteen feet away from the dung and roll the dung to their burrow. The amazing thing is, when a rotational pasture is matured, and you have a good insect population balance, dung piles literally disappear from sight within twenty-four to forty-eight hours.

Rotational grazing minimizes compaction of the soil in a pasture and makes it a more attractive neighborhood for Mr. Beetle.

Alfalfa vs. Grass

Nearly all horses prefer alfalfa hay to grass hay, but that doesn't mean you should give them a steady diet of it.

Alfalfa, or lucerne, is a perennial legume, in the same family as clover and various bean plants. Alfalfa hay is a good source of energy and protein, but not fiber. Too much alfalfa can cause hyperactivity, obesity, and even colic in horses. Australian clinician, wrangler Jayne Glenn, advises moderation:

> Alfalfa is like chocolate. I limit my alfalfa to less than 20 percent of their overall diet. They're best off with grass hay, just regular cut pasture hay. They just take a bit and go away and come back as they need it. It's like giving a child vegetables.

Grass hay, with its high–fiber content and abrasiveness on the teeth, is better for the digestive and dental health of horses. It also allows a horse to eat longer, which is good for his mental health.

Mane Purpose

The horse's mane is often the most beautiful part of his body, but it's also the hardest to maintain.

Believe it or not, a horse's mane actually serves a useful purpose, as grooming guru Susan Harris explains:

> Nature put it there to protect the horse from heat loss through the top of his neck and also to help ward off flies. They can shake their mane; their forelock keeps flies out of their eyes. But it means that it has much longer hair, much coarser hair. You have to really preserve that hair, because those long hairs tend to break off easily. And then you wind up with sort of a short, raggedy, bushy mane.

How do you protect the mane? Shampoo and condition it like you would your own hair, and be extra careful when you encounter tangles. Work through them gently, preferably using your fingers. To protect the mane during turnout or in the stall, you can always make your horse wear a spandex hood. He'll look pretty silly, but that's a small price to pay for a model mane.

Grooming the Mane

Some people spend a lot of time and money bathing and conditioning the manes on their horses. Does that really help?

Fact number one: Everybody wants to ride a good-looking horse. One of the most attractive features on any horse is a long, flowing, luxuriant mane. So how do you get that? It's partly hereditary, partly diet, and partly grooming. Susan Harris is a respected riding instructor and grooming expert. She explains why cleaning and conditioning the mane makes a difference.

> The shaft of the hair will get little irregularities that catch on things, and that's what tends to make the hair snarl and stick to things and break off. So if you can use a conditioner and a sealer that smoothes out those long hair shafts and makes them long and smooth and slippery, then they don't break off so easily and you preserve the hair you've got.

What's true for the mane is also true for the tail, which presents an even greater detangling challenge.

 ## A Pretty Tail

Want a more beautiful tail on your horse? There's more than one way to get the effect you're after.

It's common now at horse shows to see tails that are so long, so full, and so perfect that they don't look real. Welcome to the wonderful world of the tail extension, the equine equivalent of a hair weave. If you're more inclined to the real deal, there are steps you can take to maximize your horse's natural tail. A good diet, plus cleaning, conditioning, and gently detangling the tail is the place to start. Grooming expert Susan Harris offers another suggestion:

> You may want to protect the very long hair by keeping the tail in a braid, maybe covering the tail braid with a tail sack or a tail sock; this doesn't make it grow longer, but it does stop it from getting caught on things and breaking off hairs. You'd be surprised how much hair horses lose.

Brushing Benefits

When was the last time you gave your horse the brush-off? You should know that brushing does more that just remove dirt.

Brushing is not a substitute for bathing your horse. In fact, they serve different purposes. Susan Harris, author of *Grooming to Win*, says brushing puts the shine in your horse's coat.

> It stimulates the circulation. It's a little bit like the old routine where girls would brush their hair a hundred strokes every night. It also distributes the skin oil over the surface of the hair. So if you brush again and again with firm pressure, you get a little friction going. This warms it up, and you'll see the hair begin to shine, and that's because you've spread that horse's natural skin oils over the surface of his hair coat.

Always brush in the direction the hair lies. Use short, brisk strokes, no more than twelve inches in length, rather than long, slow strokes. And most important, enjoy yourself! This is quality time with your horse.

Horse Theft Update

Horses may be obsolete as beasts of burden, but 50,000 of them are still stolen each year in America.

Used to be, you could sell a stolen horse to a slaughterhouse with little trouble. Today, stolen horse alerts course over the Internet within hours of the deed, and a slaughterhouse is a good place to get busted. Add to that the growing use of subdermal microchips to identify horses, and it's no wonder thieves have had to adopt some new tactics, as writer Garth Rumsmoke explains.

> Just recently we're finding out there's an upswing in the stealing of young horses, because a horse changes his identity so quickly as he grows. So they could steal a one-week-old, and a month later, you'd never be able to recognize him. We're also finding people are stealing horses and just turning them over at a quick profit. He may be a $10,000 horse, but they'll take him down the road and sell him for $250.

By the way, those 50,000 horses stolen each year amount to less than 1 percent of America's equine population.

Showing Off Your Horse

Of course you're proud of your horse, but telling a stranger about him could be the worst possible thing to do.

There was a time when horse thieves were strung up for their misdeeds. Today, they get a slap on the wrist. Ironically, these crooks often get the unwitting assistance of their victims. Debi Metcalfe lost her horse Idaho after telling a total stranger all about her.

> Horse thieves count on the fact that people like to show off their horses, and quite often they stop and pretend that they're wanting to buy a horse, or that they're just admiring your horse because they've seen it from the side of the road. And when people don't know that horses are being stolen, most of them tell the thief everything about their animal. Two weeks before Idaho was stolen, we had that very same thing happen.

After almost a year, Idaho was recovered, but most stolen horses aren't. Now a crusader against horse theft, Debi says, "Don't talk to strangers"—at least, about your horse.

Stealing a Horse from a Pasture

Just how safe is your horse when he's out in the pasture? You may be surprised at how easily he could be stolen.

Modern horse thieves often work in teams, starting with an advance man on foot or in an inconspicuous car. Horse theft victim Debi Metcalfe explains the tactics they use.

> There's a drop-off man. He gets in the pasture, picks up the horse, and then calls for the trailer. The trailer drives up, they clip the fence, the horse is loaded, and they're gone. It's very fast and very efficient, as long as no one sees them or hears them.

By the time you notice the horse is gone, he could be halfway across the country, to a sale barn, a private buyer, or, in days past, a slaughterhouse. To be less of an easy mark for horse thieves, Debi suggests getting to know your neighbors, removing halters from pastured horses, getting a watchdog, and installing security alarms and lighting on your property.

Brand Inspection

Hot branding is still a popular way of identifying cattle in the West, but alternatives are being used with many horses.

At one time, a horse was as likely as a cow to have a big brand on his hip. To discourage theft, government agents routinely inspected brands, and if you couldn't prove you owned a horse in your possession, well, you know what they did to horse thieves. Trail riding correspondent Garth Rumsmoke talks about brand inspection today.

> Brand inspection's got a lot of people worried because they figure, "My horse isn't branded—what do I do?" Well, you don't have to have your horse branded to have a brand inspection. Brand inspection is actually just a way of proving that that horse belongs to you; that's what a brand inspector does.

Registration papers, hauling cards, or other official documents that adequately describe the horse are usually sufficient today. Freeze brands are more common now than hot brands, but the real future of branding is the insertion of a microchip just under the skin in the horse's neck.

Dead Leased Horse

Got extra horses? Need extra cash? Leasing them could be a good idea, but you need to be careful.

When a leased car is totaled, the wreckage can be kept around until an investigation is done and insurance claims are filed. Not so when a leased horse dies. For health reasons, the body must be disposed of, and this puts the owner at risk for rip-off schemes. Antitheft activist Debi Metcalfe explains.

> In a lease, quite often the owners are contacted and they're told that the horse has died. And what proof do you have that the horse has died? One of the things that I have in my lease is, if this horse dies, I have to see the horse. They cannot dispose of the horse themselves.

Whether faking a horse's death or stealing it out of a pasture, the horse thief today is often a sophisticated criminal with a network of accomplices. Our best defense is understanding how they work, and taking every possible precaution.

Wearing Teeth Down

Just because a horse's teeth need attention from us, don't get the idea that the design is bad.

When he's born, a horse's teeth are already formed—up to five inches in length—and hidden deeply in the jaw. As he grows, the teeth slowly move out of the jaw. If the teeth are not worn naturally through his diet, they should be filed down to avoid creating sores and chewing problems. Equine dentist Todd Williams, from Alberta, Canada, elaborates:

> The original design of a horse's teeth was to allow him to eat grass. Grass has a special skeletal structure inside each blade that is made up of silica or silicates, and that's something that provides a lot of abrasion to the teeth. That's why we needed to have a design that would give us lots of crown to work with, to last the horse over a period of years.

At an eruption rate of one-eighth of an inch per year, a horse's teeth could last him up to forty years.

The Speculum

When an equine dentist brings out the tools of his trade, be prepared for a nasty-looking device called the speculum.

Wild horses keep their teeth in shape by grazing almost continually. At times they chew on things considerably more abrasive than grass, like bushes, bark, or even rocks. But domestic horses don't get that sort of abrasion, and need their teeth filed down occasionally. Equine dentist Todd Williams describes the tool that makes that possible:

> The best speculums are designed to hold onto the horse's incisors (or front teeth), which sit on a set of plates. Then the operator asks the horse to open his mouth, and the speculum is used to follow that mouth open; then, it simply holds the horse's mouth in a position where we can work on the teeth.

To the layman, a speculum is a bit archaic in appearance, and while it looks like it would be uncomfortable for the horse, it isn't, because there's no leverage applied. Horses have been accepting speculums without a fuss for more than two hundred years.

Horses Helping Dentists

What's your least favorite thing to do? For many people, it's going to the dentist—but horses don't seem to mind.

It's no wonder that dentists often suffer from depression; most of us hate to see them. But the equine dentist usually has more willing and helpful patients, as Todd Williams explains.

> Horses don't seem to be nearly as bothered. In fact, in a lot of cases, horses know what their problems are, and if you provide some treatment and some help for them, they'll even halfway look like they're assisting with the treatment. They kind of lean on the float and look like they're sort of enjoying the whole procedure, as long as you're not bumping their gums or rubbing on their cheeks.

The float is a rasp used to file down the sharp points that develop through normal wear on a domestic horse's teeth. Wild horses keep their teeth in shape with a rougher, woodier diet, and when they need a little extra abrasion, wild horses will chew on rocks.

Pulling the Tongue Out

The horse's tongue is an important organ, but it has traditionally suffered more than its share of indignities.

If you're a new horse owner, grabbing your horse's tongue is probably the furthest thing from your mind; but pulling the tongue out one side of the mouth is a traditional way of propping the horse's mouth open to examine or treat its teeth. Equine dentist Todd Williams doesn't buy it.

> That's a really negative thing from a horse's perspective. I don't know of very many scenarios where I'm required to pull a horse's tongue outside of its mouth. That tongue should be left alone, and if the treatments are understood properly, there just really aren't times when it's necessary.

A horse may travel with his tongue hanging out, but it's rarely caused by overzealous tongue grabbing. Most often, he just hasn't learned yet how to carry the bit. Still, it's a good idea to have his teeth and mouth checked for signs of discomfort.

A Fat Horse's Teeth

Fat people are often stereotyped as being jolly. Fat horses are also stereotyped—as having good teeth.

Equine dentist Todd Williams spends a good deal of his time educating people about horses' teeth, and teaching horse owners how to examine them. He's found that misinformation is often the first thing he must deal with.

> The biggest misconception is that there is some correlation between the body weight of your horse and his dental well-being. The notion is that fat horses—or ones that are carrying enough body weight—can't have any dental problems. I'm pretty pudgy myself, and even I get a toothache once in a while.

The logic is sound—sort of: If a horse is chubby, he must be eating well, and if he's eating well, his teeth must be okay. But in reality, a better indication of his dental health is the horse's behavior, especially when a bit is in his mouth.

◑ Bit Seat

Like a human movie star, a top equine athlete often gets special dental care—but it's not to improve his smile.

The diet and lifestyle of the domestic horse cause his teeth to wear differently than what nature intended; thus, the need for the filing procedure known as floating. The teeth of performance horses often get extra attention to make the bit more comfortable to carry. This is called creating a *bit seat*. Equine dentist Todd Williams provides some detail:

> The idea is to actually shape and design the very front of the big grinding cheek teeth, right behind where the bit's going to sit, in a manner that radiuses them and has them come out more like your thumb, so to speak—rounded and radiused and smooth—so that the interaction of the bit and the soft tissue is relatively benign in relation to the teeth.

This reduces the likelihood that the horse will feel any pinching, poking, or pain in his mouth related to the bit.

🐎 Wolf Teeth

In the wild, a wolf is a horse's mortal enemy. In domestication, wolf *teeth* can also be a horse's enemy.

Who knows how the term originated, but most horses have from one to four wolf teeth when they are young. At one time in the evolution of the species, wolf teeth must have had a purpose, but today, they are completely useless and have very shallow roots. Wolf teeth may fall out by the age of five to six months, but if they don't, they should be removed to avoid a painful clash with the bit, says veteran horseman Richard Shrake.

> Most of them are in the upper part, right in front of the molars, and they're quite tiny. They look like the end of an eraser. Take them out, because you'll have a nice horse really performing, and then all of a sudden, the bit hits a wolf tooth and it's like hitting him with an electric shock. It'll take one back weeks.

An equine dentist can remove wolf teeth quickly and easily with a pair of special pliers.

🐴 West Nile Virus

It was first discovered near the headwaters of the Nile River in Uganda. Now this deadly disease is in the U.S.

How West Nile virus managed to cross the Atlantic and take root in America is unknown. But the way it's been spreading since it got here is well understood, as Dr. Rob Keene explains:

> It is spread by mosquitoes. Birds are the reservoir for this particular virus. They are able to amplify or increase the viral numbers in their bodies. And then when the mosquitoes bite these birds, and then in turn bite your horse, the virus can be transmitted in that way.

In less than five years, West Nile virus has spread to every state in the continental United States. Horses that contract the disease have a 30 to 40 percent chance of dying from it, or of being euthanized. It's been fatal to less than 10 percent of its human victims.

Symptoms of West Nile Virus

Like a master of disguise, West Nile virus is often hard to recognize, and that's part of the problem.

A disease may have symptoms so distinctive that they form a fingerprint by which it may be identified. Not so with West Nile virus, the sometimes-fatal disease spread to horses and humans by mosquitoes. Dr. Rob Keene discusses the symptoms of WNV:

> Normally you'll see fever. You'll see a change in behavior, a change in attitude. The horse will become ataxic. These signs can look like rabies. They can look like Equine Protozoal Myeloencephalitis (EPM). They can look like Eastern Equine Encephalomyelitis (EEE), which is another sleeping sickness virus. They can look like flu symptoms, and so they can be confused with a lot of different things.

Knowing that you're dealing with West Nile virus doesn't mean you can cure it. Victims must ride it out, and all we can do is simply make them as comfortable as possible.

Is it Contagious?

It's front-page news and the danger is real, but West Nile virus is not as easy to catch as you might think.

"Is it contagious?" That's the first question horse owners ask about a deadly disease such as West Nile virus. Contagious diseases can spread like wildfire through a barn, because one sick horse can pass it to many others. Fortunately, West Nile virus doesn't work that way, as Dr. Rob Keene explains.

> Horses are incidental hosts or dead-end hosts. Horses do not get enough of the virus circulating through their bloodstream to be a source of infection to us or a source of infection to other horses. It requires that infected mosquitoes bite a human being or bite a horse.

Mosquitoes get the disease from infected birds, so if you find dead birds in your area, have them tested by authorities, and consider getting your horses vaccinated.

EPM and Opossums

It's the most common cause of neurological disease in horses today, and it all starts with the opossum.

Equine Protozoal Myeloencephalitis is caused by an organism carried in the feces of the opossum. Where these furry critters live, horses are routinely exposed to the organism, but most horses develop antibodies that protect them from it. When the antibodies don't do their job, EPM is the result. Dr. Stephen Reed of Ohio State University discusses the symptoms.

> It can cause brain stem problems, where they have cranial nerve deficits. They can't eat. They have a head tilt. Sometimes they can't see. Most of the time, though, it enters into the spinal cord. It makes the horse walk with a wobbling gait. They just look like a wobbler.

The opossum is a marsupial found only in the western hemisphere. It's often mistakenly called the *possum*, which is a different animal altogether that lives in Australia.

EPM and Rest

Equine Protozoal Myeloencephalitis is a serious neurological disease, but it can be cured with veterinary treatment, time, and rest.

Performance horses, whether they ply their trade at the racetrack or in the show ring, are often worked almost year-round, and that takes its toll both physically and mentally. Some people just won't give their horses a break, even when they're infected with something as serious as EPM, as Dr. Stephen Reed explains.

> In horses that are subtly affected, people continue to try to race them or show them, or do whatever they need to do, and many times you can't get the organism clear because you don't allow them enough time to get their own immune system there to finish up the job.

Experts now recommend that periods of decompression and deconditioning be built into the schedule of every performance horse, even if he's healthy as . . . well, a horse.

Rest after Traveling

On long trips, horses have their own version of jet lag, and it has nothing to do with the change in time zones.

Being in a trailer is not such a bad deal for a horse, especially if he has food, water, and another horse for company. What's hard on a horse is the traveling part, says writer and trailering expert Kathy Rumsmoke. Constantly bracing and rebalancing himself takes its toll and uses different muscles than everyday life.

> That horse is working in that trailer just as hard as if you were riding him. So if you have a five-hour drive to get to the campground, it's like you've been out there riding that horse for five hours. So give him a break and let him relax and have a good night's sleep before you get on him and put him to the trail.

Along the way, it's best to let your horse stay in the trailer during rest stops. Getting him in and out at a strange location is asking for trouble. Just standing still is rest enough.

Stress and Illness

Although it's big and strong, a horse has a relatively delicate constitution, and stress is the enemy.

Stress can come from many sources, like a demanding competition, an injury, or a general anesthetic. Even a long trip can put a horse at risk, as Dr. Stephen Reed of Ohio State University explains.

> One of the most significant stress events that we see is transportation. After a horse has been on a van for six to eight hours, if you look at some parts of his immune system, it's really suppressed. It's not working up to full potential.

To minimize stress when traveling, experts recommend rest stops every two hours, and being certain your horse drinks plenty of water. Besides compromising his immune system, stress is a common cause of ulcers and life-threatening colic.

Ulcer Effects

Statistically speaking, the majority of horses have ulcers at some point, and that can directly impact their performance.

Stomach ulcers in horses are usually stress or diet-related. But whatever the cause, the discomfort the horse feels compromises his performance. Dr. Mary Brennan explains:

> This makes it difficult for them to bring their back up, to keep their abdominal muscles strong, which are critical in any performance horse, whether it's a barrel racer or a jumper or a dressage horse. The canter is the gait that seems to be affected first, and especially flying changes, because they have to tighten the stomach muscles, everything shifts, and it causes the horse a lot of discomfort if they have ulcers.

Equine stomach ulcers are seldom life-threatening, although any problem with a horse's digestive tract is cause for concern, as the development of colic is always a possibility. Rest and water-softened hay are usually prescribed.

Good, Bad, and Ugly Stress

Like a certain 1967 spaghetti Western, stress on your horse can be good, bad, or ugly.

Dr. Mike Van Noy has researched the way horses respond to stress. He's found that stress comes in different varieties.

> Carefully, intentionally applied stress is the definition of training, so that's what I consider to be good stress. It helps get horses fit or into shape and allows them to do their jobs more efficiently. Then there's the environmental stresses, and that can be heat, humidity, stall confinement, putting horses in trailers, and shipping them long distances.

Those would be the bad stresses. Now consider something that frightens the horse and causes him to react violently. That kind of stress leads to some very ugly situations. Dr. Van Noy's company makes Advanced Protection Formula, an herb-based compound that is said to help horses cope with the physiological changes that occur during stress, without dulling their minds.

Hooves and Blood Circulation

Ever wonder why so many horses die from heart failure while still in their teens? It may have to do with their feet.

Greek horseman Xenophon wrote in the fourth century B.C. that horses could live to be fifty. Of course, he was talking about barefoot horses, whose hooves are able to assist the heart with circulation of the blood. Hoof specialist Sabine Kells explains.

> The hoof—even though it's seemingly very hard—is actually a flexible organ, and when bearing weight, it expands; when the horse's foot is picked up, it contracts a little bit again. That is the blood-pumping function of the foot, and also, it provides shock absorption.

Some believe that nailing shoes onto a horse's feet diminishes the pumping action of the hooves, making the heart work harder to circulate the blood. Over many years, the added strain may take its toll. Ironically, in spite of all the money we spend on them, horses today have a life expectancy of about half what Xenophon suggested.

Hittite Chariot Horses

More than three thousand years ago, barefoot horses were conditioned for extraordinary levels of performance.

Most of today's equine athletes wear metal shoes. But are they necessary for high levels of performance? History shows us that long before the advent of nailed-on shoes, barefoot horses were routinely worked harder than we can imagine. Hoof expert Sabine Kells offers this example:

> The earliest record that we have of high-performance barefoot horses is about 1350 B.C., where they found some Hittite cuneiform tablets and translated the very interesting regimen for training the chariot horses of the Hittites, who were contemporaries of the Egyptians at the time. They were putting between 50 and 125 miles a day on their barefoot chariot horses.

And these chariots were heavy; the wheels stood as tall as a man. It was a training regimen few horses could handle today, with or without shoes.

 **Hoof Boots**

Today hoof boots come in bright colors and space-age materials, but in the old days, they were rather crude.

Hoof boots serve different purposes. They can act like a spare tire when your horse loses a shoe out on the trail. They're sometimes used in treating hoof injuries to keep the area clean and the medicine in place. But the most common use is probably as an alternative to horseshoes, providing protection and traction for a barefoot horse working in difficult terrain. As Sabine Kells explains, early attempts at hoof boots predate nailed-on shoes by several hundred years.

> They had metal sandals for the Roman draft horses that they tied on to the horse's foot with a thong, but those could go no faster than a walk, so they were not used for the cavalry horses. For about the last fifteen years or so, it has been known that the nailed-on metal horseshoe did not come into common use until the Middle Ages.

Walking on Soles

The horse's hoof is a remarkable structure, and the more we learn about it, the less we seem to understand it.

Like most people, veteran farrier and hoof-care guru Gene Ovnicek thought horses were meant to walk on the walls of their hooves. Then he took part in a study of wild horses living in three different areas with vastly different ground conditions.

> We found that with all of the horses in this study, particularly the front part of their foot, the wall was worn down to the level of the sole, and those horses in the most abrasive terrain had virtually no hoof wall touching the ground at all. And that was surprising. It showed me very clearly that there was more to the horse's foot than I had ever perceived and realized in the past.

Rather than offering answers, the study raised more questions in the already confusing and sometimes heated dialogue about hoof care and the advisability of shoeing horses.

Mismatched Feet

Is your right foot a perfect mirror image of your left foot? Probably not. It's the same with horses.

The last time you bought shoes, the salesman probably asked, "Which is your larger foot?" and measured that one. Farriers expect horse hooves to vary in shape from breed to breed, but they, too, must contend with mismatched feet. Hoof-care specialist Gene Ovnicek explains:

> Even within those breeds, we see horses that have one foot that looks different than the other, one that's more upright than the other, and to get those two feet so they will land the same is the best for the body. There has been a big misunderstanding in our technology for years as to how to deal with these feet that are mismatched.

Gene says that 70 percent of horses today have significantly mismatched feet, probably due to both genetic and environmental factors.

🐴 Baby's Feet

If you overprotect a horse when he's a baby, you could be sentencing him to foot problems for the rest of his life.

Newborn foals appear to have identical hooves all the way around according to studies, but as they grow and exercise, the fronts and backs take on their own size and shape. If activity is limited, this development can be stunted. Gene Ovnicek is a respected farrier and hoof-care specialist who has seen the detrimental effect on the feet of show horses.

> If you look at the very special horses, the ones that are worth the most money, they're the ones with the smaller feet, and they're the ones that were probably limited in their exercise when they were foals because they didn't want to get them hurt. The culls, kicked out in the back pasture, basically the same breeding, have better feet.

And the feet are bigger, too, because that's what a horse needs. Time and again, man's interference compromises the development of one of nature's most splendid creatures, the horse.

Moisture in Hooves

Some experts claim that horses' hooves need plenty of moisture. Others say that's a mistake.

Advocates of barefooting horses recommend that hooves get lots of moisture. They say this aids in the normal expansion and contraction of the hoof, what they call the hoof mechanism. Henry Heymering is president of the Guild of Professional Farriers. He argues against this notion of hoof mechanism, and says that adding moisture is not good for a horse's feet.

> In the hoof wall, there's a moisture gradient. The inner third of the hoof wall is about 33 percent moisture, the middle third about 25 percent, and the outer third about 15 percent. The hooves need that gradient in order to work properly. So when you moisturize the outside you're ruining that gradient and destroying the effectiveness of the hoof wall.

Heymering believes the hoof functions more like a rigid cylinder with a moving piston inside, and that this action is what helps pump blood back to the heart.

Wild vs. Domestic Horses

Researchers study the wild horse to learn more about the needs of the domestic horse. But are they really the same?

Take a grungy, free-ranging feral horse and put him next to a spotless, pampered show horse. The differences will be obvious, but according to horse care expert Sabine Kells, these are purely superficial.

> They are the same species, they are the same animal—because what is the wild horse in North America but a domestic horse that has managed to escape the care of man? And vice versa; you take the wild horse and you bring them into domestic living conditions, and within six months they experience all the same lameness and health problems that our domestic horses experience.

In spite of all we do for our horses, their wild cousins are usually hardier, healthier, and happier. Thus, the growing interest in providing domestic horses with more natural boarding environments. Ironically, once we let nature do its part, horsekeeping becomes easier.

Pasture-Raised Horses

There's no doubt about it. A well-planned barn makes life a whole lot easier for anyone with horses, but barns are primarily for the convenience and comfort of humans. Healthy horses actually grow stronger by living outdoors, as endurance riding legend Julie Suhr explains.

> Horses, by nature, were intended to roam all over and run away from predators, and that develops their natural ability, their physical ability. If a horse is stalled, he simply does not have that opportunity to exercise his body.

Horses don't need stalls, but they do need shelter from wind and rain. Natural terrain provides that for the wild horse. For the pasture-raised horse, a run-in or loafing shed is recommended. Most important, let his coat grow wild and free. That's nature's way of keeping him warm and dry.

 **Run-Out Pen**

Are you worried that your barn is too drafty for your horses? Well, chances are, it's not drafty enough.

What we like in our homes is not what's best for horses. A barn should have plenty of outside air circulating through it, even when it's cold. Natural horsekeeping advocate Sabine Kells takes it one step further.

> Have somebody cut a door in the outside of the barn so that the horse can not only come into the central stall aisle and be taken in and out that way, but also, it can have a little run-out pen on the outside of the barn and, hopefully, a run-out pen that is shared by other horses.

When you come right down to it, barns are mostly for the comfort of people. Nature has given the horse a sophisticated thermoregulation mechanism that keeps him comfortable in weather that would kill us. But he must use it or he'll lose it. There's nothing wrong with providing shelter for your horse; just be sure he also has access to the great outdoors, and of course, to other horses.

Four Perfect Places

Of all the places in the world you could raise horses, two of the most perfect are right here in America.

A horse does best with a diet of high-quality, high-fiber forage; in other words, hay or pasture. Pasture is generally the better of these two because it takes longer for the horse to eat and keeps him on the move throughout the day. Experts call this natural grazing behavior. But not all pastures are created equal, according to equine reproduction expert Karen Berk:

> There are four perfect places in the world to raise horses with the absolute perfect limestone-based grass. And those are: Newmarket, England; Chantilly, France; Lexington, Kentucky; and Ocala, Florida.

Ocala's year-round mild climate makes it the most ideal, and the sheer size and diversity of the horse industry there have earned it the title Horse Capital of the World.

Horsekeeping in Germany

Germans love their horses as much as anybody else, but many have a serious problem: lack of space.

Ideally, a horse should be able to run free in a large pasture with a group of his buddies. If that's not possible, regular turnout in a good-sized paddock is recommended. But in some parts of Europe, like Germany, for instance, even that can't be done, says clinician GaWaNi Pony Boy.

> People here would be absolutely amazed at how little space they have to work with their horses. Many of the horses in Germany are in stalls, or in the riding ring, and that's it. They never see the light of day. They don't have paddocks or corrals or any of those things. There's just no space to do it.

Europeans are beginning to embrace the concepts of natural horsemanship, and they're beginning to understand how to deal with the behavior problems caused by isolating horses and confining them in stalls virtually around the clock.

Gelding Late

If your mare is in foal, now's the time to make a decision about gelding the baby. You have all the information you need.

Unless a male foal has really outstanding bloodlines, he should be castrated immediately after birth. But some owners put off this simple procedure for years. The result is a gelding that acts like a stallion. Clinician GaWaNi Pony Boy explains:

> I dealt with one a few months ago in Germany, where I just would have sworn it was a stallion. I could not believe it was a gelding horse because it was terribly aggres-sive—snorting, spitting, doing all those stallion character-istics, going up and striking—and it had been gelded at ten years old. Of course, they're individuals. Some are going to be worse than others. But if you know it's going to be a gelding, tomorrow's the best.

Even for an adult horse, gelding is a simple procedure that can be done while the horse is standing in his stall. A sedative is given to make him groggy, and a local anesthetic eliminates any pain. In a few days, he's fully recovered.

Too Little Time

Some people buy a horse for fun and relaxation, only to find out that it adds stress to their lives instead of taking it away.

Boarding your horse and taking riding lessons at a local stable may seem an ideal low-stress way to get into horse ownership. But for folks who are already busy, a rather joyless routine often emerges, according to clinician Dan Sumerel.

> They grab the horse out of the stall, they brush him off real quick, shove a carrot in his mouth, say hi, pet him a little bit, put the saddle on, ride him out, warm him up in a hurry, because their lesson starts in four minutes. They ride around, somebody yells at them, "Heels down, heels down" for thirty or forty-five minutes, or an hour. Then they get off the horse, they brush him off again, they take the saddle and everything off, they put the horse away, they give him another carrot, and they go home.

They're missing so much! The real joy of horse ownership comes when your horse lives with you and you interact with him every day. Daily chores like feeding and cleaning stalls can be fun and relaxing.

CHAPTER SEVEN

Breeds

Origin of the Saddlebred

In America's first century, the horse we now call the American Saddlebred enjoyed widespread popularity because of its smooth riding gaits. As time went on, regional differences developed when breeders sought to enhance the gaits that best suited their terrains, leading to offshoots like the Tennessee Walking Horse and Missouri Fox Trotting Horse. But where did the granddaddy of gaited horses, the original Saddlebred, come from? According to historian Lynn Weatherman, it started with an old New England breed, now extinct, called the Narragansett Pacer.

> The idea was to improve the so-called "native stock," and the basic American Saddlebred came about with crossing Narragansett Pacer mares on Thoroughbred stallions.

The Saddlebred was originally known simply as the Saddle Horse.

Rex the Saddlebred

Although mostly a show horse today, the five-gaited American Saddlebred has a rich history as a real "using" horse. It was the favored mount of Civil War officers, including Lee, Grant, Sherman, and Jackson, as well as working cowboys heading west after the war. In the 1960s, producers of Disney's adventure series, *The Swamp Fox*, also selected a Saddlebred to carry their dashing young star, Leslie Nielsen, who reminisces about his equine co-star.

> Rex was the name of the beautiful black American Saddlebred horse. They were standing him then, too. He couldn't run—they're not bred for running—but he was five-gaited, and you could throw him into a rack or God knows what. It was like sitting in a rocking chair.

The double horse for Rex was a black running horse owned by saddle bronc legend Casey Tibbs.

Fox Trot Gait

The fox trot may be the first dance step you learned, but it's also the signature gait of a very popular breed of horse.

Its ancestors include the Saddlebred, Standardbred, Morgan, Tennessee Walker, and Arabian, but the Missouri Fox Trotting Horse has its own identity, defined primarily by its fox-like shuffling gait, a gait with a rather distinctive rhythm. Trainer Gale Thompson describes it:

> When the horse is actually doing a fox trot, we use the cadence *chunk of meat and two potatoes, chunk of meat and two potatoes*. That's the actual cadence. It's a broken gait. Durability and stamina is what the fox trot comes in for.

A Fox Trotting Horse is also extremely sure-footed, versatile, and gentle. But the biggest reason for its popularity is the smoothness of that gait. Riders float along as if on a magic carpet, without the trauma and trepidation of the traditional trot.

Fox-Trotting Cow Horse

When it comes to working a cow, the Quarter Horse rules, but other breeds do a respectable job, too.

The desire to control a cow is part of a horse's genetic programming, and it isn't limited to just Quarter Horses. Gale Thompson trains Missouri Fox Trotting Horses, and notes that the foundation bloodlines in that breed also produce cow horses.

> You go back to your old Zane Grey–type breeding. These horses were used daily to work cattle. All of our young colts, when we're breaking them, we use them on cattle, just to get them out and get them down and break them. And we find that the Missouri Traveler, going back to the Zane Grey–bred horse, they can't help from looking at a cow.

With the right kind of training, a horse's interest in cows can be channeled into a specific skill, such as cutting, reined cow horse, or roping. And if he's not destined for the show ring, a horse with cow sense may still make a good ranch horse.

Too Many Gaits

Novice riders have enough to worry about just staying in the saddle, so it's no wonder some of them don't show much interest in gaited horses.

Remember when you were first learning to ride a bicycle? You probably didn't have a whole lot of interest in a ten-speed English racer right then. It's the same with horses. Today's gaited breeds require a more experienced rider to fully appreciate their capabilities. Missouri Fox Trotting Horse trainer Gale Thompson explains:

> They may have five, six, seven, sometimes more different gaits that they can do, and the novice has a hard time of determining, not only how to get them in this certain gait, but how to hold them there. So this is probably one of the drawbacks, and why people sometimes hold back on riding a gaited horse.

But they really shouldn't. With a little bit of instruction, beginning riders can soon master the basics. Best of all, with these gaited breeds, there's no trot, and that really smoothes out the road.

 **Broken Gaits**

A horse that moves with a broken gait is not defective. In fact, its broken gait makes for a smoother ride.

Before there were roads, nearly everyone traveled ahorseback, and the "ambling" or gaited horse was preferred. Instead of a jarring two-beat trot, the middle speed on these horses is a comfortable four-beat or broken gait, where each foot touches the ground separately. Some breeds, like the Missouri Fox Trotting Horse, can do more than one broken gait, says trainer Gale Thompson.

> You have what the old-time farmers called the single foot. You have a running walk; you have a rack. These are all different variations of speed and footwork, but the fox trot is the main gait, and that's what they're bred into. Ninety percent of them will do the natural fox trot.

The regular trot and the pace are not comfortable gaits to ride because the horse is jumping back and forth from one pair of legs to the other.

Paso Fino in the U.S.

Columbus, the conquistadores, and American soldiers. They all played a part in getting the Paso Fino to America.

More than five hundred years ago, on Columbus's second voyage to the New World, about twenty-five Spanish horses were pushed overboard to swim to shore at Santa Domingo. They were adopted by the conquistadores, refined, and used as remounts. Over time, these horses we now know as Paso Finos became extremely popular in Puerto Rico. Former Paso Fino Horse Association vice president Al Berry picks up the story.

> After World War II, a lot of the GIs coming back to the States actually started bringing the horse to the U.S. and the visibility of the Paso Fino from South-Central America to North America started at that point, after World War II.

Paso Fino means "fine step," and refers to the short, quick stride that distinguishes the breed's ultrasmooth gait.

Artificial Insemination for Thoroughbreds

They're born and bred to be the best running machines on earth, but some say Thoroughbreds could be better.

Thoroughbred owners want to breed their mares to the best stallions available. Yet because they're not allowed to use artificial insemination, it's logistically difficult and expensive to access new blood. They lose the proven benefits of hybrid vigor, and they wear out the good stallions they do have, as reproduction expert Karen Berk explains.

> When I watch a stallion being bred six days a week, three times a day, to the point where his libido goes "I don't want to do this anymore," I look at it as almost a humane issue. I have the utmost respect for the Thoroughbred industry, but AI would definitely simplify the workload.

Equine transport companies and others that benefit from the current ban on artificial insemination will undoubtedly continue to fight its acceptance for Thoroughbreds.

Reasons to Freeze

The Byerly Turk, King, Secretariat . . . If these great stallions were alive today, we could make them immortal.

The business of freezing stallion semen is just that—a hugely important and profitable business. Besides providing global access to the finest regional bloodlines, frozen semen is a way for a stallion to continue siring sons and daughters long after his death. And according to reproductive consultant Karen Berk, it's surprisingly inexpensive.

> It's much less money than showing a horse or buying a saddle. We've really taken it to a whole new economic level. There are certain genetic lines that are leaving us, and to be able to perpetuate that is incredible, because then you can get into line breeding thirty years from now and bring these lines back in, which strengthens a breed.

Unfortunately, the use of frozen semen and artificial insemination have not yet been accepted by the Thoroughbred industry.

 **Asking Questions**

When it comes to buying a horse, you need to be as nosy as a busybody neighbor to get the kind of horse you want.

Who, what, where, when, and why. You should have a barrage of these kinds of questions ready whenever you consider buying a horse, regardless of its age or intended use. Author Sharon Smith counsels people on buying horses for retraining. She offers this advice:

> Owners vary in how much they'll tell you, but assuming that they'll be honest, just ask everything you can think of about how the horse is trained, how he behaves, what he does. And perhaps there, if you're looking specifically to retrain, you may get some ideas about the background he has and the likelihood that his characteristics will suit what you hope to do with him.

Remember, the only dumb question is the one you don't ask! And remember to get that prepurchase exam from a reputable equine vet. The questions you ask the vet could be the most important of all.

The Questioning Mule

The mule is half horse and half donkey, and if you don't understand how his mind works, he can be all trouble.

Living side by side in the mule's brain are the often-conflicting sensibilities of the horse—a run-first, think-later panic-aholic—and the donkey, a think-first, fight-if-you-have-to situational analyst. Depending on the mule's disposition, his analytical side can simply challenge the trainer to be his best, or it can make his life a living hell. Mule trainer Steve Edwards elaborates:

> A mule is always questioning everything, and you need to answer that question. If you've got a disposition where that mule would rather argue with you than go ahead and complete the discussion properly, then you're going to have some problems.

A young mule's disposition is determined largely by the disposition of its mother, the mare. She passes it on genetically and through her interaction with her foal.

Blue Moon, the Mother Mule

Mules are a hybrid species, a cross between a horse and a donkey.

With its odd number of chromosomes, the mule should not be able to reproduce. However, there have been isolated cases down through history where female, or molly, mules have given birth. Mule trainer and breeder Steve Edwards talks about the most famous such case, a molly mule with a very fitting name.

> The one that sticks out in my mind, that most mule riders are aware of, is a mule called Blue Moon. Sometime in the '50s, she did produce a mule colt—one, one year, and one a second year. And she was actually bred by a horse.

Why did this molly become a mommy? No one seems to have an explanation. The other unanswered question is how many fertile mules have gone undetected over the years, simply because conventional wisdom and science said that attempting to breed them was a waste of time.

Haltering a Mule

Mules must be trained the way horses should be trained, and how they react to haltering proves the adage.

When it comes down to it, horses are pretty forgiving creatures. They tolerate ignorance and insensitivity from us humans remarkably well. By contrast, mules don't suffer fools, and if you want to get along with them, you need some mule sense. Mule trainer Steve Edwards offers an example—something as simple as haltering the mule.

> When you start walking into that corral, Mr. Mule's going to tell you what his day's going to be like. And if you take the time to pet him, rub him really good, then slide the halter on, everything's done nice and quiet and then put away the same way. The way you put that mule up will be the way you can take him out the next day.

A mule's questioning nature is often misinterpreted as stubbornness. Give a mule time to figure things out and he'll go the extra mile for you.

A Mule's Sensitive Nose

The most distinctive feature on a mule's head is certainly the ears, but it's his nose that trainers really use.

Mule fanciers are quick to point out the differences between the mind of a mule and its short-eared cousin, the horse. But physically there are numerous differences, too, some of which affect how they are best trained. For example, the bit, which is so common in controlling horses, is not nearly as effective with mules, according to mule trainer Steve Edwards.

A mule cares more about his nose than he does his mouth. He'll take that old mouth and get a hold of that bit and take you anywhere he wants to take you. But when it comes down to his nose, that nose is extremely sensitive. I can get more done with a rope halter and a hackamore in a shorter amount of time if one has not been touched than I can with a snaffle bit.

These devices allow pressure to be placed on the bridge of the mule's nose.

Mules as Guard Animals

Mules suffer from a certain stereotype: the stupid, often stubborn beast of burden. They're not.

If you're accustomed to the look and behavior of the horse, you may need a little time to appreciate all the good points of the mule. The result of mating a female horse and male donkey, mules have characteristics of both species. One thing we hope the mule gets from his donkey dad is the tendency to stop and think in scary situations rather than just run away. As Duane McPherson, former executive director of the American Miniature Horse Association, explains, donkey-minded mules can make good watchdogs.

> Some people are using mules as guard animals for the miniatures. You know, in areas where they have bears or wolves or coyotes that could mess with a smaller animal, they'll keep a mule right there along with them.

Sheep ranchers sometimes keep donkeys with their herds for this same purpose. Try doing that with a horse!

Breeding Quarter Horses

Today's Quarter Horse breeder faces a real challenge if he wants to win in the show ring.

There's a saying among people who raise horses for a living: You breed the best to the best, then hope for the best. Chance plays an undeniable role in how a foal comes out, but smart breeders know how to stack the odds in their favor. Quarter Horse breeder and world-champion Western performance horse trainer, Al Dunning, discusses his strategy:

> Basically, I'm looking to breed the contemporary horse to a foundation kind of mare, or vice versa, and it's better to stick with the horses that are winning out there. I'm too old to try and reinvent the wheel. So if you tell me you've got a Smart Little Lena out of a Bueno Chex mare, or something like that, I'm going to want to ride that horse.

Still, the dream of every breeder is to stumble upon the magic outcross, a new bloodline that can add hybrid vigor to a breed and take it to an even higher plane.

The Problem with Bulldogs

Early Quarter Horses were shorter and more heavily muscled than you see today, and they had an unflattering nickname.

By 1950, the descendants of sires such as Steeldust and Old Billy dominated the Quarter Horse breed. They were affectionately known as *bulldogs* because of their solid, compact build and protruding jaws. But breeder Walter Merrick felt they could be improved. His son, Joe Merrick, explains:

> A lot of people were just compounding that compactness to a point where horses weren't able to do much other than rope calves or do things in the arena. And, having worked on ranches all his life, he realized that, while those horses might be valuable in the pen, they wouldn't help you much as the day wore on if you were out trying to work cattle or get something done. So not only was he trying to find horses that could go down the racetrack a little farther than 220 yards, but he also knew that those were just better horses overall.

Merrick's solution was to introduce the blood of a special Thoroughbred stallion, the now-legendary Three Bars.

Walter Merrick and Three Bars

Today's Quarter Horse is faster, taller, and more athletic than his ancestors, thanks to Walter Merrick and Three Bars.

Walter Merrick made a name for himself racing bulldog-type Quarter Horses like Midnight Jr. and Grey Badger II. Although his horses were blazingly fast for 350 yards, he felt they slowed down too much after that. So Walter made the controversial decision to add Thoroughbred blood, betting his future on an unknown eleven-year-old stallion named Three Bars. Merrick biographer Frank Holmes describes the impact of this decision.

> Because of Walter's reputation as one of the great match racers in the Southwest, when he imported Three Bars to western Oklahoma in 1952 and bred him to seventy mares—including mares owned by some of the greatest breeders in the area—that literally redirected Quarter Horse evolution.

The modern Quarter Horse owes much of its versatility to Three Bars.

Why Three Bars?

At a time when the country was filled with Thoroughbred racehorses, one was selected to improve the Quarter Horse breed.

The pedigree of virtually every modern Quarter Horse contains names with *Bar* or *Bars* in them. This is in homage to the Thoroughbred stallion that was used to refine the breed in the 1950s. Quarter Horse breeder Walter Merrick was looking for a very special Thoroughbred stallion when he found Three Bars. Author Frank Holmes reveals Merrick's criteria.

> It could not be just any Thoroughbred. It had to be a horse that he felt could be functional as a cow horse as well. It had to be a medium-height horse, a horse with good long muscle. And the minute he saw Three Bars, he told me, he knew that he had found the horse.

Besides the desirable physical characteristics, Three Bars was a kind, gentle horse with an excellent disposition. Crossed on the great bulldog lines, he produced Quarter Horses that were larger, more athletic, and extremely versatile.

Ranch Horse

If you just want a good horse and don't care about pedigrees, look for a veteran ranch horse. You won't be disappointed.

They may not be as fancy as show horses or as fast as racehorses or as strong as draft horses, but for all-around usefulness, ranch horses are hard to beat. Horse trainer and clinician Curt Pate specializes in the ranch horse. Here's how he defines it:

> It's a workhorse. It's a horse that is used in a situation to do a job, which is handling cattle. And he might be roped on. He might be cut on. He's kind of an endurance horse, making the big circles, covering a lot of country.

Making the big circles means riding the perimeter of an area where cattle are spread out and driving them back to a central area. It takes a tough, sure-footed horse to do that kind of work, one with a good head on his shoulders and a solid work ethic. The ranch horse is gaining in stature, and competitions are being organized to feature them.

Grullo Horse

Its body is mouse-colored, it has a dorsal stripe, and tiger-like markings on its legs. It's called a *grullo* horse.

The grullo is not a breed, but a color type often mistakenly grouped with duns, buckskins, and palominos. Although it usually has a gray-brown look to it, a grullo horse is quite different from a gray horse, which has a mixture of white hairs with darker hairs. Author Lisa Wysocky offers further clarification:

> If you look at a grullo-colored horse, the hair is all the same color. Genetically, the grullo horse is very similar to a black horse, and there is what they call a dominant dun factor gene, called the D gene, that kind of washes the black out to a grullo kind of shade.

In some areas, *grullo* (GREW-yo) is considered the masculine form and *grulla* (GREW-yuh) the feminine. The word is rarely pronounced correctly. Incidentally, grullo derives from the Spanish word for a gray crane, a steel-gray-colored bird.

Miniature Horses

They are bred and shown with as much enthusiasm as any breed of riding horse, but they're half as big!

Enter the Alice-in-Wonderland world of the miniature horse, where everything looks normal, only smaller. The first record of miniature horses comes from Europe about four hundred years ago, when they were playthings for the children of royals. Later they were put to work in Welsh coal mines. Today, miniature show horses have been refined to look identical in conformation to their full-sized counterparts, says former American Miniature Horse Association executive director, Duane McPherson.

> That is the entire object of this. If you have a picture with nothing in it that helps you determine the dimensions of the animal, you would not be able to tell the difference between a large horse and a miniature horse.

To be registered in the AMHA, the horse must have recognized bloodlines and be no more than thirty-four inches tall at the withers.

Gaited Morgan Horse

Is America's beloved Morgan horse a smooth-gaited trail horse or a fast-trotting show horse?

In 1789, Vermont businessman Justin Morgan acquired Figure, a bay yearling colt that would become the founding sire of a new American breed, and immortalize his owner's name. Versatility has always been the hallmark of the Morgan horse, and that extends to its way of moving. This has led to some interesting rules for showing them, as gaited horse specialist David Lichman explains.

> The Morgan Horse Association has a rule that, in the horse show, the horse should not show any tendency toward a smooth gait in the show ring. And the mere presence of the rule indicates there is a tendency in the bloodlines; in fact, the early Morgan horses were primarily gaited horses and smooth to ride.

Good trainers are able to bring out the smooth four-beat lateral gait of the Morgan, a gait that makes trail riding a real pleasure.

Riding a Standardbred

Since Colonial times, the breed we know today as the Standardbred has been a harness horse. But what about riding them?

As a harness racing horse, the Standardbred is taught to trot or pace, and never to canter. Instead of the chiseled features valued in other breeds, the Standardbred has a drooping face, with a "Roman" nose. So why make him a riding horse? Retraining expert Sharon Smith offers a compelling reason.

> It's probably the easiest thing in the world to teach a Standardbred to ride, because they are the best-natured horses. I can't say enough about Standardbreds. I love them. They make terrific riding horses because they are so used to being handled. Now, of course, they've never had a rider on their back, and it's the nature of a horse to think that anybody on his back is a predator who wants to eat him up. But you know, they're so easygoing that it's a pretty quick process to do it.

Once a Standardbred understands that it's okay to canter, he can perform that gait like any other horse.

The Market for Geldings

A top breeding stallion can be a money machine, but there's still a lucrative market for good geldings.

Professional horsemen agree that there are too many stallions in the horse industry. Most are not active breeding animals because they're not high enough quality. For trainer and breeder Al Dunning, the answer is simple: Geld 'em.

> A great gelding can be a horse that I could put ten or twelve people on, and you all could get along with him. But I guarantee you, take that stud, and there might not be any of you who could get along with that particular stud. So that just opens the market for a lot more people by gelding that horse.

Gelding, or castration, is a quick, relatively simple procedure that can be done with a sedative and a local anesthetic, often while the horse is standing. Raising good geldings can be good business. They can sell for thousands, tens of thousands, and sometimes, hundreds of thousands of dollars.

CHAPTER EIGHT

Anecdotes

My Mom's a Goat

Ready for a feel-good story? Here's the creative way a Canadian horseman handled the problem of an orphaned foal.

Tia the foal had lost her mother to colic shortly after birth, so for breeder Glen Wutzke and his wife, that meant round-the-clock bottle feedings. A suggestion from their vet sparked a laborsaving idea.

> He called and said goat's milk was a very close second to the mare's milk, and if we could find a goat to milk, then we could supplement with milk from the goat. So when we got the goat, we just sort of took it a step further, and thought, well, we'll try putting the young horse onto the goat. It worked quite well.

Millie the goat quickly accepted Tia's nursing, and would even climb onto an overturned sleigh to make herself easier to reach. Tia flourished, and the Wutzkes slept through the night. The Tia and Millie story has been documented in a video called *My Mom's a Goat*.

Buck and Ladybird

The Diamond Spur Rodeo in 1969 was a big break for pint-sized performers, the Idaho Cowboys.

As eight thousand fans looked on, Bill and his brother Dan, better known as Smokie and Buckshot, galloped into the arena, ropes in hand. Suddenly one of their matched pinto ponies broke formation and bolted, with six-year-old Buckshot frantically pulling on the reins.

> Ladybird hits the brakes and I go shooting over her head like I'm shot out of a cannon, do a perfect somersault in the air, and I land on my feet. I was stunned by this, but I looked down and my rope was still in my hand. The whole place was quiet. So I just started spinning my rope.

Like his airborne dismount was part of the act! Needless to say, the crowd went wild. Today, he's a horseman and trick roper known around the world, but Buck Brannaman still believes that was his finest performance.

 **Mabel Todd**

She was a physical therapist whose pioneering work affected the course of riding in the twentieth century.

In 1921, therapist Mabel Elsworth Todd of Boston began working with an eight-year-old girl afflicted with a curvature of the spine. Todd gave her not only exercises but also a new way of looking at her body, says author Susan Harris.

> Mabel Todd taught a lot about how bodies work, how anatomy functions. She also taught using mental imagery. Instead of just telling you to stand up straight, she'd say, "Walk as if you had a hook from your head to the clouds." And that was before her time in the 1920s.

Todd also encouraged the girl to ride. In spite of her handicap, the girl excelled, and later incorporated much of Todd's work in an innovative approach she dubbed Centered Riding. Today, ninety-one-year-old Sally Swift is still quick to credit her condition and her teacher for her success.

Orren's Quarter Horse

Orren Mixer's famed painting of the ideal Quarter Horse still sparks debate. Which horse was it?

An artist in great demand, Orren Mixer was working on seven different portraits of living horses at the time he committed to canvas his image of the ideal Quarter Horse. It was a fabrication—Orren's personal vision of a good compromise between the bulldog Quarter Horse and the Thoroughbred.

> You don't have that perfect horse. I've painted horses that had faults, that were the greatest when it came to performance. Then I've looked at horses that are like perfect statues, but a lot of them can't do anything, or they don't have the brains or something. They're like people.

The controversy over this painting arose when three of the seven owners for whom Orren was then painting claimed that their horses were his model. Not true, says Orren; although he does admit that certain body parts of real horses may have slipped into his work.

Roy Clark's Fear

He's one of America's most celebrated entertainers, but Roy Clark was nearly defeated by a horse.

As a young man, country singer and guitarist Roy Clark played as hard offstage as on, and he paid the price. One of his worst injuries occurred when a horse reared and fell on him, crushing his leg. Recovery took eleven months, and it was four years before he faced a horse again, this time at a friend's ranch. Nashville publicist Lisa Wysocky relates what happened next.

> The friend put him in a round corral with a new yearling colt. The colt took one step toward him and his heart started thumping and he was sweating and just had this panic attack. It was all he could do to get out of the round corral and get away from the colt.

It took another year of mental exercises and visualization for Roy to overcome his equiphobia, but he did it, and went on to become a respected breeder of Quarter Horses and winning Thoroughbreds.

Robert Vavra's Unicorn

It was an experience some Colorado schoolchildren will never forget: coming face-to-face with a unicorn.

Celebrated equine photographer Robert Vavra had completed a long day's shoot when the snow began to fall. Suddenly invigorated, his photographic model broke free and began a headlong gallop down the mountain, a blur of white against the pine trees.

> And just as it got to the bottom of the hill, on this really out-of-the-way, rural road, a school bus came around the curve. The driver slammed on his brakes, the kids jumped out, and there they were, face-to-face with this unicorn, with a mane that was a yard long, steam coming out of its nostrils . . .

And a single horn protruding from its forehead, courtesy of the special effects department. Who knows what parents thought that evening when they heard the story of this close encounter of the magical kind.

 **Walter Farley**

He could spin a yarn with the best of them, but behind author Walter Farley was a real horseman.

His horse stories have thrilled generations of youngsters and helped to instill in them a passion for reading that schoolbooks often don't. But few people know that the late Walter Farley left us nonfiction books on his favorite subject, too. Carol Alm, president of the Black Stallion Literacy Project, elaborates:

> He also wrote a couple of other books on horsekeeping, horse training, and horse care. His philosophy way back then, interestingly enough, parallels the philosophies today of John Lyons, Pat Parelli, and Ray Hunt.

But Walter Farley is best remembered for his twenty-five books starring the Black Stallion. Still popular after sixty years, these timeless stories are now the backbone of the Black Stallion Literacy Project, a privately funded effort to promote reading among grade-school children.

Swamp Fox Spills

In Disney's 1959 television series, *The Swamp Fox*, Leslie Nielsen's stunt double earned his keep.

For the stuntman, it had not been a good day. That morning while galloping across a swamp in star Leslie Nielsen's place, he had been pitched headlong into the water when his horse stumbled. Now he and the horse faced an even harder swamp stunt. Leslie remembers watching from the sidelines, along with the head wrangler for the series, a quiet old cowboy named Fred Guest.

> He'd get to a bank on the other side and the horse is going up, and, boy, the horse can't make it. The horse goes straight up and back over. So, that double's in the drink again. And Guest is up there, you know, and he's sort of chewing on his tobacco, and he says, "Yessir. He's sure getting to be a clown, ain't he?"

Chances are the bedraggled stuntman, whose name is lost to history, didn't see the humor. That's Hollywood!

Bill Dorrance, the Teacher

His insights redefined modern horsemanship, but Bill Dorrance also had a unique ability to teach people.

He was always eager to talk horses with anyone experiencing a problem, and buried within Bill Dorrance's simple, sometimes cryptic comments were truths that enriched those who dug them out. He was a rancher and horseman by vocation, but he had the soul of a teacher, as clinician and Dorrance friend Mike Beck explains.

> He was available to help. He loved to help people. In fact, he told me one time, "You know, if I'd never had a ranch and a family, I would have really enjoyed having a school . . . to help people."

Even without a school, the Dorrance style of gentle horsemanship caught on, and is now taught around the world. Known as natural horsemanship, its central goal is to make your idea the horse's idea, so that he willingly and eagerly does your bidding. And yes, much of this works with kids, too.

Trailering in Europe

If you were a horse owner in Europe, you'd find things a bit different, especially when traveling with your horse.

In America, we've grown accustomed to seeing one-ton dually pickups pulling massive multihorse trailers with living quarters. You don't see that in Europe. High gas prices and high taxes on vehicles that guzzle too much of it encourage a different type of rig—and also staying closer to home, as clinician GaWaNi Pony Boy observed.

> First of all, they have trailers that are outfitted for cars. A little Datsun can pull these trailers because they're made of canvas with aluminum tubing. The second thing is, horse shows are within a couple miles of your house.

But what if your horse is too big for the Datsun and your destination is too far for riding? You do have a third alternative—a commercial equine transport service. If you've got the money, honey, they've got the time.

Getting a Horse to Clinic

Having trouble loading your horse into a trailer? There are clinics to help, but you do have to get your horse there.

Horses are claustrophobic by nature, and prone to panic when forced into tight spaces. This is why they must be trained to go into a horse trailer. The training itself isn't difficult to master; in fact, just getting the horse to the clinic is often the bigger challenge. Some owners ride their horses. Others turn to more drastic measures. Monty Roberts talks about a horse brought to one of his trailer-loading clinics.

> I had one in San Diego one time that they knocked out on a tarpaulin. Got about six guys and slid it into a stock trailer, and when it woke up, it was at the building site at about eight in the morning. And then they had the rest of the day to let the anesthetic wear off. He's on our *Load-Up* video, that one.

The goal in this type of training is to cause the horse to *want* to be in the trailer.

Training in the Circus

As a kid, did you ever consider running off and joining the circus? Well, you might have been surprised at the work involved.

Tanya Larrigan was born into a circus family. Her parents were master animal trainers, and little Tanya was especially good with horses and ponies. But it was traditional and economically necessary that all circus children learn as many skills as possible.

> For all the children, you went through every single thing to see in the end which way you could specialize. Because if you think about it, at school you do a variety of subjects and then find where your niche really stood. Realistically, you have to be able to turn your hand to more than one thing. And most of the artists would be able to do another act of some description.

Today Tanya is a respected horse trainer and outspoken advocate of the use of voice commands with horses, an idea that's generating a lot of interest in Europe and the U.S.

Black Stallion Literacy Project

Kids, horses, and books. It's the Black Stallion Literacy Project's recipe for success.

The Black Stallion Literacy Project uses Walter Farley's Black Stallion books and hands-on experiences with real horses to get kids excited about reading. President Carol Alm describes the program:

> It's not about teaching phonics and teaching reading as much as it is about providing a motivating factor. We did 35,000 kids this year in ten different states, and all of the anecdotal evidence indicates that's absolutely what happens. You put the kid in touch with a horse, whether it's a first grader or a fourth grader, and they get very excited about reading.

The Black Stallion Literacy Project is a joint effort of Walter Farley's family and the owners of Arabian Nights, an Orlando family dinner theater with an equestrian theme starring . . . you guessed it. The Black Stallion.

Horses on Airplanes

Many of today's top competition horses are international jet-setters just like their riders.

The mythical winged horse Pegasus is a fitting symbol for today's best performance horses. Air travel is a necessity for these equine athletes, and most handle it surprisingly well, due in part to their in-flight accommodations. Olympic gold medalist David O'Connor explains.

> It's almost like a horse trailer without wheels. You load the horses on the ground and then they ship that whole pallet up into the plane. For the horses, I think, in a lot of ways, it's easier than being in a trailer, because they don't get bounced around. It's just the takeoff and landing. You have hay with them all the time. If it's a combi flight, which is half passengers and half cargo, you can be with them for everything but takeoff and landing.

This is another good example of the adaptability of the horse. Nothing in nature could prepare him for the sensation of flying through the air.

Early American Horses

Long before Europeans came to North America, horses existed here. Then they mysteriously disappeared.

Linda Little Wolf is a Native American historian and horse-woman. She has studied the impact horses had on her ancestors, the Plains Indians, and what her research has taught her may surprise you.

> The horse is not native to this country. Ten thousand years ago, the modern-day horse, *Equus caballus*, disappeared entirely from the North American continent. Many historians believe it was a result of the Ice Age. Many of these herds managed to migrate to Asia via a small land bridge that connected the two continents at that period of time.

It wasn't until the 1500s that horses were reintroduced to North America by Spanish explorers. But what about those original American horses? Well, chances are it's their descendants that have helped make China the horsiest country on the planet.

Tanya's Shetland Pony

Many adult horse lovers today had an experience as a kid with a Shetland pony . . . and lived to tell about it.

At the age of five—eight years before her singing career took off—country superstar Tanya Tucker's dream came true: Her dad gave her a Shetland pony, by the name of Pretty Boy. Unfortunately, Pretty Boy turned out to be pretty bad.

> He'd go up underneath these trees and rake me off, and he about broke my back several times. I guess the final straw was when I was leading him in front of the house and my dad was looking out the big plate-glass window there, and that little pony reared up and started to paw me. I mean, my dad came out there and took that lead rope and led him to town, which was a couple miles away, and sold him right then.

Shetland ponies today have shed much of their negative image due to better breeding, training, and management. Like any other horse or pony, they can be taught to be docile and compliant, and to be a good mount for a child.

David's Gold Medal

It's the ultimate symbol of athletic achievement, but David O'Connor's Olympic gold medal has a rough life.

His individual gold in eventing at the 2000 Olympics in Sydney was just one more in a long string of international awards for American horseman David O'Connor. And it was not the first Olympic medal he or his wife, Karen, had won in eventing. So, the medal took on a life of its own.

> You should see it; it's beat to death. We just give it to people, so every scratch and dent represents somebody, instead of locking it into a safe, where it's really not very useful. It's not only a part of us, but the actual token of it, I think, is a very American thing, and a very people thing. So, Pony Club kids come in the house all the time and they're putting the medal on and stuff. That's the way it should be, I think.

David and Karen O'Connor use and endorse natural horsemanship, and have proven through their success that it works for high-level performance horses as well as for companion animals.

🐴 Lap Horse

Many people like the companionship and small size of a lap dog, but what about a lap horse?

When full grown, a miniature horse can be up to thirty-four inches tall at the withers and weigh four hundred to five hundred pounds—about half the height and weight of a standard riding horse. As a baby, a miniature horse is cute and cuddly, resembling a child's stuffed animal, and can easily be lifted by a human. Duane McPherson is former executive director of the American Miniature Horse Association. He tells of one owner who found her baby mini a little too irresistible.

> This lady had a little rocking chair out there in the barn, and she had gotten into the habit of rocking this foal. It's now a two-year-old, and it still keeps trying to crawl up in her lap.

That two-year-old mini weighs about 150 pounds. That is a lapful of horse!

Circus Horse

Do you want to experience the ultimate in equestrian skill, athleticism, and artistry? Try the circus!

Circuses were, and still are, precision operations featuring truly amazing animal and human talent. From the circus's earliest days, horses have been part of the show, according to dressage clinician Mari Monda Zdunic.

> Prior to competition dressage, horses were used for entertainment in Europe. Even in our country, our best dressage prior to, let's say, 1950 would have been in the circuses, where people would take a horse that did all the Grand Prix movements as we know them, and do them in a thirty-three-foot circus ring.

Perhaps the most colorful and crowd-pleasing of all horse exhibitions is *high school* dressage, best represented by the leaping, bounding, and rearing of the world-famous Lipizzaner stallions doing their "airs above the ground."

Stunt Injury

Even with specially trained horses and exceptionally athletic riders, movie stunts are dangerous.

For rodeo bronc rider Danny O'Haco, Hollywood stunt riding seemed like an easy and fun way to make a buck. After, all, he did know how to fall off a horse! So when a chance meeting turned into a golden opportunity, Danny went for it, eventually appearing in more than twenty theatrical and television movies. Then, when he least expected it, he got hurt.

> One time in Santa Fe, I went to get on the horse, and my spur hung in the blanket of the saddle and the horse went to bucking. I went over but my leg stayed on, so I got drug down the path a ways. Luckily, the spur broke and I came off, but I crushed a disk in my neck. It ended my career as a stunt guy.

But it didn't end Danny's enthusiasm for the movie business. He recovered and continues acting today, mostly on the ground.

Stunt Preparation

A Hollywood stunt rider is part athlete, part actor, part daredevil, and sometimes, part con artist.

In the film business, you have to always be ready for your Big Chance. Former stunt rider Danny O'Haco grabbed every tough riding assignment he could get. "Sure, I can do that!" he'd say, secretly hoping he could work it out before the cameras started rolling. It took guts and some real riding chops. Luckily for Danny, the horses usually knew what they were doing.

> There are different cues and different things for each horse. The owner that trained the horse needs to be there to give you a little lesson on that kind of stuff. A lot of times, you have thirty minutes to learn everything you need to know.

It wasn't always about falling off the horse, either. In a Budweiser beer commercial, Danny galloped through a campsite, leaned down, and snatched a bottle of beer off the ground—all without spilling a drop. For Danny, it was just another day at the office.

🐎 Stunt Horses

On the silver screen they may look like regular horses, but in Hollywood, even the equine actors are specialists.

From its beginning, the motion picture industry has had a love affair with the horse, but the last thing a director wants on his set is an unruly equine. Trainers of movie horses are thus highly respected for their expertise, and stunt riders like Danny O'Haco bet their lives on it.

> If you're working on a lot of movies, you don't have the time to train horses, so there are people that do this for a living, and then they lease their horses out to the stunt people to ride. That would be a horse that does a specialty, like a falling horse or a rearing horse, or a horse that's trained to go without his bridle. You know the horses are good horses because they're smart, and if you have horse savvy, you usually get along pretty well with them.

Some movie horses are specialists at standing still, and sometimes they have to do it for hours at a time.

Pony Express

If you were an orphaned, teenage boy in 1860, there was one job custom-made for you: Pony Express rider.

Perched atop leather mailbags, the young riders of the Pony Express raced across America's landscape and right into its history books. The dangers and hardships they faced were formidable, but so was the pay. Surprisingly, given the near-mythical stature the Pony Express attained in later years, it was not long in operation. Author and horse trivia expert Lisa Wysocky fills in the facts:

> Actually it was about eighteen months. It started in April of 1860 and stopped in October of 1861. During that time they carried 35,000 letters, and the route covered almost 2,000 miles.

It was the transcontinental railway that ended the Pony Express. With the start of the Civil War, railroad construction was fast-tracked, and even before all the tracks were laid, mail routes were being taken over by trains.

Tanya's Cutting Career

She was a singing sensation at thirteen, and by then, superstar Tanya Tucker was also a serious horse lover.

She was a tomboy who loved the rural life, especially if horses were around, so when she reached adulthood, country singer Tanya Tucker decided to once again make horses a part of her life. This time it was cutting horses.

> I truly love it. Unfortunately, I've never really been able to focus a lot on it. I have this other gig I do that takes me away. But you know, it's also enabled me to be able to do these celebrity events that are a lot of fun.

Tanya has competed against celebrities like Joe Montana, Christie Brinkley, Johnny Rutherford, and Kix Brooks. And she holds her own; in 1991 she won the National Cutting Horse Association celebrity cutting event. It was a good year for Tanya Tucker. She also gave birth to a son, and won the Country Music Association's Female Vocalist of the Year Award.

Buck and the Movie

Buck Brannaman was the main inspiration for the book *The Horse Whisperer*, and he also kept the movie real.

When novelist Nicholas Evans sold the movie rights to *The Horse Whisperer*, he recommended that director Robert Redford use Buck Brannaman as a technical consultant. Redford did, and was stunned to hear the changes Buck felt were necessary to keep the horse scenes accurate and the rest of the dialogue believable.

> We had a lot of meetings where we'd go over that script word for word. Cowboys and ranch people kind of have a language of their own. If you tried to sound like you were a rancher or cowboy and you knew nothing about it, you wouldn't be convincing. So we spent a lot of time working on it over the next year or so, and wrote a bunch of things and got it done.

The horse industry overwhelmingly embraced the movie for its authenticity, and at the same time got a little chuckle over the Hollywood touches that even Buck couldn't keep out.

Vaqueros Swapping Horses

The rich history of California horsemanship is preserved in the lore of the *vaquero*, Spanish for "cowman."

Central California during its colonial period was a vast grazing empire. The men charged with managing the valuable herds of beef cattle developed their own system of horsemanship, which is known today as the vaquero, hackamore, or California system. So respected were these horsemen that sharing finished horses among them became somewhat commonplace, as trainer R.E. Smith explains.

> They say that the vaquero never walked anywhere, that he galloped a horse from point A to point B at all times. And it was so much so that ranchos would have a line of horses, so that when a vaquero rode from one ranch to the other, which might be a day's ride, there would be horses spread out for him to be able to get on. He would just leave a finished horse and grab a new one and take his ride.

By the way, the Spanish word *vaquero* was adapted by Anglo cowboys, and came out "buckaroo."

Vaquero Training Schedule

If you are ever tempted to rush the training of a young horse, take a lesson from the *vaqueros* of old California.

These days, many horses are started in training too young, brought along too quickly, and ruined before they've even reached maturity, all in the pursuit of winnings at the track or the show pen. As appalling as that might seem to us, it would be inconceivable to the master horsemen of old California, the vaqueros. Modern vaquero R.E. Smith elaborates:

> The vaquero had tens of thousands of horses to choose from. The horses that were picked showed the highest promise as far as the way they were built and the way their minds worked. They really didn't even look at a horse until they were four or five years old, and mature. And then when they did pick a horse, they spent the time with them. It would take four to five years for them to go from the *jaquima* to the *freno*, which is from the hackamore to the bit.

So a finished bridle horse was eight to ten years old; compare that to racehorses that are pushed to the max at two.

Jockey Eddie Arcaro

It's easy to get discouraged when success is slow coming your way. If that happens to you, just think about Eddie Arcaro.

Leaving school at fourteen to ride Thoroughbreds, George Edward Arcaro launched a thirty-year career in which he won nearly five thousand races, and purses totaling more than thirty million dollars. At his retirement, *Sports Illustrated* magazine called Arcaro "the most famous man to ride a horse since Paul Revere." Eddie passed away in 1997 at the age of eighty-one, but he lives on in the record books. Author Lisa Wysocky lists some of his accomplishments:

> Eddie Arcaro is the only jockey in history to have won two Triple Crowns. He rode all the big horses of the 1950s and '60s and '70s, like Citation and Nashua and Kelso. And he went on to win five Kentucky Derbies, six Preaknesses, and six Belmont Stakes.

Even more impressive, Eddie Arcaro had 250 *losing* rides before he won his first race.

Sioux Indians and Horses

They were hunters, farmers, and fighters. And the Sioux Indians of America's northern plains were also horsemen.

Horses were an integral part of daily life for the Sioux, or Lakota Indians. They had three distinct types: transportation horses, hunting horses, and war horses. Their riding abilities were astonishing, and the acrobatics they would perform on horseback during a buffalo hunt or a skirmish are rivaled today only by top rodeo trick riders. But as Lakota Sioux historian and horsewoman Linda Little Wolf explains, the mighty Plains Indians were not a horse culture for as long as you might think.

> The horse was acquired by the Sioux in 1770. By 1890 we were all confined to reservations. We still had horses, but we were no longer the great horse culture living that life.

One hundred twenty years may seem like a long time, but remember—horses have been domesticated for six thousand years.

Orren and the Kids

He's one of America's most beloved painters of horses, but Orren Mixer's work has suffered some real indignities at the hands of kids.

In 1956, New Mexico horseman Punch Jones commissioned up-and-coming artist Orren Mixer to paint a portrait of his prized racing mare, Maroon. The big oil painting was displayed lovingly in the Joneses' home. But one Saturday, while Mom and Dad were on their weekly trip to town, the four Jones boys got a little rowdy, and the painting of Maroon the mare took an arrow right through the heart. A distraught Punch Jones turned to the only person he thought could save it—the painting's creator, Orren Mixer.

> I took it home and got some linen and string and sewed up that hole. I fixed it up a little bit and painted over it. He's got it back on the wall now. I hope they haven't shot any more holes in it. Oh, they were just a bunch of good kids. I've raised four boys. Every one of them painted on my pictures. There was one of them used the same color I did, and it took a long time to even notice it.

Leslie's Famous Dismount

Hollywood stars and their horses have doubles to do the dangerous or difficult stunts . . . most of the time.

When a lead actor is injured, it can throw an entire film off schedule, so producers just don't take chances with the welfare of their stars, human or equine. But accidents can still happen, especially when there's lots of action. Actor Leslie Nielsen remembers one such occasion in filming the 1960s Disney series on Revolutionary War hero Francis Marion, the Swamp Fox.

> I'm known for one of the most famous dismounts as Francis Marion. I rode up to the log cabins and I ran in. Now, when you get off a horse, before you can run you have to get your foot out of the stirrup, and I started to run with my foot still in the stirrup, so I took the fall.

His famous dismount aside, Leslie is a fine rider, with a life-long love of horses that he shares with his daughters.

Squires

In medieval times, knights had assistants that helped them with their horses, tack, and armaments. They were called squires.

Matthew Mansour is part of a jousting troupe known as The Order of the Brass Monkey. The troup's presentations are part history lesson, part circus act, and all entertainment. Although the knights get the glory, the squires keep things running smoothly. Matthew offers further insight on the squires of days past.

> A squire during the period would have been a child presented to the knight from another nobleman, to train to become a knight. Even during the period, some people never achieved knighthood, and they were squires well into their fifties and sixties. It was not something that was looked at as bad. It was just a career path that they chose.

Modern squires serve as ground crews for the armor-clad knights. During shows, they move props in and out of the arenas, reset targets, and keep a keen eye open for problems that the knights can't see. They must also be adept at handling horses and driving big trucks.

Blindfolded Rope Tricks

Rope tricks are hard enough to do while standing on the ground with both eyes open. But not for the Idaho Cowboys.

World-renowned horseman Buck Brannaman is also an accomplished trick roper, and he's been spinning his loops since he was a kid. It was his brother, Smokie, the other half of the Idaho Cowboys, who came up with the twist that made their ridin' and ropin' act really special: doing a trick blind-folded. Their promotion-minded father thought they should take it a bit further.

> First thing you know, he has us doing about 90 percent of our rope tricks blindfolded, which I hated doing. But it made a pretty good show. We would do a Texas skip, for example, standing in the saddle on the back of our horse. A Texas skip is a trick where you spin a vertical loop and you jump back and forth through it.

The learning curve on that trick brought its share of bumps and bruises. Buck advises youngsters not to attempt it today without putting some padding on the ground first.

Indian Horses in Battle

American Indian warriors had something every trail rider today covets: a truly bombproof horse.

Nothing is worse on a trail ride than a horse that spooks too easily. Now, if you're going into battle with a horse, it's even more important that he remain calm and focused on you. Linda Little Wolf explains what her ancestors, the Lakota Sioux Indians, put their war horses through.

> Many times warriors would dismount suddenly and go into hand-to-hand combat. In the middle of a huge battle-field, with bows and arrows flying and guns going off, that horse would remain within eight feet of its rider, waiting for the voice command to run up and allow the warrior to remount his horse. These horses were pretty much bombproof to what was going on around them. They were trained for that. They had one focal point: the rider.

War horses were prized possessions that were guarded carefully, as they were always in danger of being stolen.

Shaking for Claimers

One way to acquire a racehorse is the claiming race, but you may need a little luck along with your loot.

The principle behind the claiming race is simple: You commit just before the race starts to buy a certain horse for a set price, regardless of how he will place in the race. Any owner or trainer registered with that track has the same chance to claim the horse, and sometimes more than one person does. So who gets the horse? Racehorse trainer Janet Del Castillo explains:

> If two or three people put a claim in on the same horse, they do what's called a *shake*. If there are three people, they'll put balls numbered one, two, and three into a bottle. They'll shake it and they'll pull out number two, and if you're number two, you get the horse.

So in racing, not all the gambling takes place among spectators. There's often action on the backside as well, where successfully claiming the right horse can become a horseman's claim to fame.

Why Trotting Horses?

Turn back the clock a couple centuries and you'd find most people rode gaited horses. What happened?

Early Americans preferred smooth-riding gaited horses that allowed them to cover a lot of ground without wearing out horse or rider. So how did trotting horses, often called "bone shakers," gain a foothold? Gaited horsemanship instructor David Lichman provides some answers.

> Throughout history, there were some places where the shift was made over to trotting horses; in the middle of the eighteenth century in the dressage ring, for instance. And there was also the invention of the *posting trot*. They call it the post because the postal riders would carry the mail on the back of the horse, and they would find that they could go faster if they trotted. They "posted" (stood slightly in the stirrups on alternating strides) to keep from getting jarred so much as they traveled down the roads.

As roads improved, trotting, already preferred for driving horses, became accepted for riding as well. It seems our ancestors were in a hurry, just like we are.

Redford the Horseman

Actor Robert Redford has performed several notable movie roles on horseback, but what kind of horseman is he?

Butch Cassidy's partner, the Sundance Kid, mountain man Jeremiah Johnson, and the Electric Horseman, Sonny Steele—these roles proved that, like most actors of his generation, Robert Redford could ride a horse. But it was his role as Tom Booker, the "Horse Whisperer," that suggested he might have the stuff to be a real horseman. Working cowboy and trainer Curt Pate served as technical consultant on the film.

> I really admired him, and I really respected what he wanted to do. He watched, he listened, he tried, and just like that, he picked things up. He's a very natural athlete and he could be a good horse trainer, because he's soft, but he wants to get things done, and he's just real observant.

And of course, no one looks better in a cowboy hat than Bob. Redford also directed *The Horse Whisperer* and relied heavily on Curt and fellow clinician Buck Brannaman for authenticity.

Will Rogers's Roping

He's remembered as an author, lecturer, movie star, and humorist, but before all that, Will Rogers was a roper.

Standing in front of an audience, beloved American humorist Will Rogers would often chew gum and do rope tricks as he commented on current events, business, government, and people. But long before he took to stage and screen, Will was a working cowboy with unusual rope-handling ability. One of his early movies was built around that theme. Remarkable even by today's standards, that film made a particular impression on two young trick ropers, Buck Brannaman and his brother, Smokie.

> An old movie called *The Ropin' Fool* by Will Rogers was a real inspiration to us. We basically copied as many of Will Rogers's rope tricks as we possibly could.

At the Will Rogers Museum in Claremore, Oklahoma, *The Ropin' Fool* is played in slow motion to show how Will's ropes took on a life of their own.

Coronado and the Indians

For the American Indian, life changed forever in 1541 when Coronado brought the horse into the colonies of New Mexico.

At the time, Native Americans were nomads, eking out a meager existence on foot. Naturally, they were fascinated with the horses brought by the famed explorer Coronado and his men. Lakota Sioux historian and horsewoman Linda Little Wolf offers more detail.

> Generally, they were Spanish Barbs and a little-known agricultural horse called a Sorraia, which was a very small horse used in the fields and for pulling agricultural wagons. Coronado forbade the trading of horses to the native people, but he did hire them to work with horses. And this was the first time an Indian met a horse.

Rather than invent a new word for these marvelous, highly useful animals, the Indians simply called them *big dogs*.

A Bamboo Pole and a Square Pen

How do you gentle a wild horse? One increasingly popular method uses a square pen and a bamboo pole.

For much of his eighty-six years, Oregon horseman John Sharp has gentled wild horses with his own, somewhat unorthodox methods. So when the first annual Wild Horse Workshop was held in 1997, John was invited. Clinician Frank Bell relates what happened:

> The first day, everybody kind of went out and demonstrated their particular technique. There were some people doing conventional round pen. Some people were roping. John goes in there with his bamboo pole and makes us all look silly. In an hour, he's got these horses just completely gentled out. Five years later, two-thirds of the people are doing the bamboo pole; it is so unbelievably effective.

John used the bamboo pole to caress the horse from a safe, nonthreatening distance, until he could replace the pole with his hands. He did it in a square pen, where the horse was likely to seek comfort in a corner, instead of running around and around.

Performance Potential

Beware of the young horse that is claimed to have "perform-ance potential." Too often, that means nothing.

Champion Quarter Horse trainer Al Dunning can pick winners as well as anyone, and even he is sometimes fooled about how a horse will turn out. Like with a recent cutting horse futurity prospect that showed tremendous ability at first, but simply lost interest in the work as the training intensified. Disappointed and a little puzzled, Al pulled her out of competition.

> Now, I had another one that had been plodding along, and I kept thinking, "Come on, you're not enough horse," and he just kept taking an extra step every now and then, getting better and better and better, and I ended up winning about $60,000 on him.

The moral of this story is that horses react differently to the rigors of training. For some, it brings out the best; for others, the worst. Performance potential is a long way from a sure thing, so don't bet the farm on it.

Appendix

Contact Information for Guests Quoted

NAME	TELEPHONE	WEB SITE
Clinton Anderson	888-287-7432	www.clintonanderson.net
Doug Babcock	785-675-3080	www.dougbabcock.com
Mike Beck	831-484-2810	www.mikebeck.com
Frank Bell	800-871-7635	www.horsewhisperer.com
Karen Berk	352-465-8881	www.frozen-semen.com
Roger Braa	509-968-9167	www.teampenningnorthwest.com
Buck Brannaman	—	www.brannaman.com
Peggy Brown	419-865-8308	www.anatomyinmotion.com
Chris Cox	940-327-8113	www.chris-cox.com
Peggy Cummings	800-310-2192	www.peggycummings.com
Charles de Kunffy	—	www.charlesdekunffy.com
Janet Del Castillo	863-229-8448	www.backyardracehorse.com
Paul Dietz	623-742-7285	www.pauldietzhorsemanship.com
Stan Dill	800-260-7072	www.saddlebums.com
Al Dunning	480-471-4600	www.aldunning.com
Steve Edwards	602-999-6853	www.muleranch.com
Kirsten Farris	—	www.equestrianathlete.com
David Genadek	507-498-3668	www.aboutthehorse.com
J.P. Giacomini	859-339-3474	—
Jayne Glenn	+61 3 5777 3831	www.wranglerjayne.com
Julie Goodnight	719-530-0531	www.juliegoodnight.com
Dr. Temple Grandin	—	www.templegrandin.com
Lendon Gray	—	www.dressage4kids.com

NAME	TELEPHONE	WEB SITE
Van Hargis	903-383-2160	www.vanhargis.com
Kenny Harlow	434-983-2221	www.kennyharlow.com
Clay Harper	719-539-4332	www.clayharperinc.com
Susan Harris	607-753-7357	www.anatomyinmotion.com
Frank Holmes	785-598-2368	www.loftent.com
Chris Irwin	877-394-6773	www.chrisirwin.com
Jaime Jackson	870-743-4603	home.alltel.net/star
Nancy Jaffer	—	www.nancyjaffer.com
Jessica Jahiel	217-684-2570	www.jessicajahiel.com
Bob Jeffreys	845-692-7478	www.bobjeffreys.com
Martha Josey	903-935-5358	www.barrelracers.com
R.E. Josey	903-935-5358	www.barrelracers.com
Mike Kevil	—	www.startingcolts.com
Bob Kiser	877-788-7253	www.kisermfg.com
Gayle Lampe	573-392-4395	www.williamwoods.edu
Tanya Larrigan	—	www.larrigan-equestrian-promotions.com
David Lichman	916-648-1004	www.davidlichman.com
Linda Little Wolf	352-237-2847	hometown.aol.com/nativevisions8
John Lyons	970-285-9797	www.johnlyons.com
Josh Lyons	970-285-9797	www.joshlyonstraining.com
Ken McNabb	307-645-3149	www.kenmcnabb.com
Debi Metcalfe	704-484-2165	www.netposse.com
Dr. Robert Miller	—	www.robertmmiller.com
Tom Nagel	815-858-4090	www.zenandthehorse.com
David O'Connor	—	www.oconnoreventteam.com
Gene Ovnicek	719-372-7463	www.hopeforsoundness.com
Lynn Palm	800-503-2824	www.lynnpalm.com
Linda Parelli	800-642-3335	www.parelli.com

NAME	TELEPHONE	WEBSITE
Pat Parelli	800-642-3335	www.parelli.com
Curt Pate	—	www.curtpate.com
GaWaNi Pony Boy	—	www.ponyboy.com
Bryan Pulliam	877-744-6150	www.grazierfence.com
Monty Roberts	888-826-6689	www.montyroberts.com
Garth Rumsmoke	—	www.garthandkathy.com
Kathy Rumsmoke	—	www.garthandkathy.com
Jane Savoie	—	www.janesavoie.com
Mike Schaffer	—	www.mikeschaffer.com
Blane Schvaneveldt	714-826-5584	www.schvaneveldtranch.com
Louise Serio	508-835-8813	www.ahjf.org
Richard Shrake	541-593-1868	www.richardshrake.com
R.E. Smith	530-824-3511	www.resmithtrainer.com
Julie Suhr	831-335-5948	www.endurance.net/juliesuhr
Dan Sumerel	800-713-5861	www.sumereltraining.com
Dr. Mike Van Noy	877-661-3505	www.auburnlabs.com
Robert Vavra	—	www.robertvavra.com
Chester Weber	352-895-1139	www.chesterweber.com
Don West	800-821-3607	www.donwest.net
Anna Jane White-Mullin	—	www.annamullin.com
Charles Wilhelm	510-886-9000	www.cwtraining.com
Todd Williams	403-933-2036	www.equinedental.com
Wayne Williams	317-745-1466	www.illinoishorsefest.com
Richard Winters	805-640-0956	www.wintersranch.com
Glen Wutzke	306-668-5675	www.saskatoontruckparts.ca
Lisa Wysocky	—	www.powerofhorses.com
Mari Monda Zdunic	810-632-5725	www.shineabit.com

About the Author

Rick Lamb is the host of two nationally syndicated radio programs, *The Horse Show with Rick Lamb* and *The Horse Show Minute*. He has conducted more than 1,000 interviews with trainers, instructors, clinicians, competitors, veterinarians, and other horse experts. His programs have won six national awards.

As a writer, Mr. Lamb has to his credit more than 800 radio commentaries, hundreds of broadcast commercials, a monthly magazine column, and one prior book, *The Revolution in Horsemanship and What It Means to Mankind*, coauthored by Robert M. Miller, D.V.M. (The Lyons Press, 2005).

Mr. Lamb was born and raised in Wichita, Kansas, and holds a BS degree in mathematics and philosophy from Wichita State University. Since 1977, he has been the proprietor of Lambchops Studios, a commercial audio recording facility that serves as home base for all of his activities. A professional musician since the age of fourteen, he still performs when time allows.

Rick Lamb resides in Arizona with his wife, Diana. They have three grown children, three horses, and a cat.